NEXT GENERATION FINANCE

ADAPTING THE FINANCIAL SERVICES INDUSTRY
TO CHANGES IN TECHNOLOGY, REGULATION
AND CONSUMER BEHAVIOUR

Edited by
ROBERT LEMPKA AND **PAUL D. STALLARD**

HARRIMAN HOUSE LTD

3A Penns Road
Petersfield
Hampshire
GU32 2EW
GREAT BRITAIN

Tel: +44 (0)1730 233870
Email: enquiries@harriman-house.com
Website: www.harriman-house.com

First published in Great Britain in 2013.

ISBN: 9780857193476

British Library Cataloguing in Publication Data
A CIP catalogue record for this book can be obtained from the British Library.

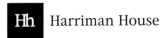 Harriman House

CONTENTS

INTRODUCTION

If any good has come out of the 2007-2009 financial crisis, considered by many to be the worst since the Great Depression in the 1930s, it must be the realisation that the financial service industry will never be the same again. It is time to stop harkening back to the days when you would, without question, trust the people who helped you with your money.

Companies operating in the financial services sector in the UK, across Europe and throughout the world must be serious about earning the trust and loyalty of customers. They have a job on their hands because they face a wiser, more knowledgeable, more demanding consumer. A consumer who has been repeatedly hurt and left jaded by the events of recent years.

If there is to be a road map for the future of financial services in general, and banking in particular, it is probably best illustrated by comments from two of the clearest thinkers on this subject. The first is Professor Julian Franks who, in his evidence to the Parliamentary Commission on Banking Standards, said "What we need to avoid a similar crisis (recent financial crisis) is structural change."

Second, Sir David Scholey, for many years one the City of London's top merchant bankers, when asked to comment on the recent financial crisis, said "Large numbers of people, myself included, were taking responsibility for businesses they did not understand." Sir David went on to say that after Big Bang in 1986, many leaders found themselves running banks which undertook activities that were beyond their comprehension. They trusted others to run these activities and when the banks became even bigger and more complicated this inherent flaw became a fatal weakness.

Many of us learned from our teachers that the best way to solve a complicated problem is to break it down into small pieces and solve each piece one at a time. The idea behind this book is very similar; we have invited experts in their respective fields of the financial services sector to illustrate the most likely route ahead. We hope you enjoy reading their thoughts and pick up some useful signposts to help you take the right path for you and your business in the future.

Robert Lempka

Paul D. Stallard

FREE EBOOK VERSION

As a buyer of the print book of *Next Generation Finance* you can now download the eBook version free of charge to read on an eBook reader, your smartphone or your computer. Simply go to:

http://ebooks.harriman-house.com/nextgen

or point your smartphone at the QRC below.

You can then register and download your free eBook.

FOLLOW US, LIKE US, EMAIL US

@HarrimanHouse
www.linkedin.com/company/harriman-house
www.facebook.com/harrimanhouse
contact@harriman-house.com

1

CHANGE IN THE FINANCIAL SERVICES SECTOR – CHALLENGES AND EFFECTS

MONEY LAUNDERING REGULATORY AND COMPLIANCE REGIMES

BY MARTIN CHEEK

ABOUT THE AUTHOR

Martin Cheek has been at the forefront of anti-money laundering (AML) regulation and the development of electronic solutions to automate AML Compliance since the first regulations in 2004. As a qualified lawyer he has a detailed understanding of the overriding regulations and the way they are interpreted by the various regulatory bodies.

Martin was instrumental in developing one of the earliest electronic verification systems in 2004; as the lead executive he set up Callcredit Direct to deliver this early electronic AML verification service. By 2008 the business had over 3000 clients in the Legal, Accounting and Financial Services Sectors. The awards won by the technology included the Legal Technology Awards 2009 Online Product of the Year.

Subsequently Martin joined SmartCredit as managing director and became a data partner of Experian, building a new anti-money laundering verification system known as SmartSearch. Using the very latest technology and the best available reference data, this system uniquely delivers both individual and business AML verification all in one platform. This new platform has over 500 client firms and over 2000 users. SmartSearch won two awards in 2013 before it was formally launched in June.

INTRODUCTION

TECHNOLOGY HAS NO doubt had a massive impact for financial institutions and banks over the last 30 years. With an ever-increasing global market, technology has empowered these organisations to move money internationally in seconds. Whilst these technologies bring major benefits they also create opportunities for money launderers and for criminal financing activity. Illicit funds can be washed through the international financial system, allowing criminals clean funds to invest in legitimate businesses or property, or to finance organised crime and terrorism.

WHAT IS MONEY LAUNDERING?

Money laundering takes many forms, including:

- trying to turn money raised through criminal activity into clean money (this is *classic* money laundering);
- handling the benefit of acquisitive crimes such as theft, fraud and tax evasion;
- handling stolen goods;
- being directly involved with any criminal or terrorist property, or entering into arrangements to facilitate the laundering of criminal or terrorist property; and
- criminals investing the proceeds of their crimes in the whole range of financial products.

THE SCALE OF THE PROBLEM

The scale of the money laundering issue can scarcely be exaggerated. Estimates have to be treated with caution, but the International Monetary Fund (IMF) estimated over ten years ago that the aggregate size of money laundering was anywhere between 2% and 5% of the world's gross domestic product. For the United Kingdom, an estimate by HM Treasury was that the most serious forms of organised crime alone generated an illicit turnover of some £15 billion a year, leading to money laundering through the regulated sector – banks, insurers, accountants, lawyers and the like – of £10 billion a year.

The Financial Conduct Authority (FCA) – which took over responsibility for overseeing the financial markets in April 2013 following the break-up of the Financial Services Authority (FSA) – has warned that its analysis of 17 banks found that half, including four major UK lenders, still did not have proper processes and procedures for ensuring they were not involved in facilitating money laundering.

Tracey McDermott, head of enforcement at the FCA, said that banks' trade finance businesses remained particularly vulnerable to abuse by criminals and terrorists and that in some cases the shipments being funded by lenders were just "fresh air". "Some banks have a lot of work to do to raise their game to the best of their peers," said Ms McDermott.

Martin Wheatley, chief executive of the FCA, warned that organised criminal gangs "filtered, cleaned and rebottled" £10 billion in the UK every year, using banks and other financial services. "It's simply not acceptable for firms to turn a blind eye to where the money comes from, its journey from A to B," said Mr Wheatley.

ACTION THAT HAS BEEN TAKEN

HSBC was fined a record $1.9 billion (£1.3 billion) by US regulators in 2012 for its involvement in illegal money laundering – this saw Britain's largest bank implicated in aiding Mexican drug cartels and breaking sanctions with Iran.

Standard Chartered was also fined $327m for its involvement in financing trade with Iran, as well as other countries subject to US sanctions, such as Libya and Sudan. Lloyds Banking Group and Barclays have also been fined for breaches of anti-money laundering rules.

In the case of HSBC, the bank only narrowly avoided facing criminal prosecution after signing a controversial deal with US prosecutors to avoid any further punishment. The deal led to criticism that large banks were "too big to jail" after senior regulators in the US and UK admitted that it could harm financial stability to prosecute a major lender.

Ms McDermott did not single out any banks, but said a "deep dive" into the anti-money laundering process had found breaches of the rules. "We are still too often left disappointed by what we see," she said.

Among the cases cited by the FCA was a scrap metal deal financed by a bank between a British Virgin Islands-registered company and a business in United Arab Emirates which saw the metal traded without any documents showing who was taking delivery of it. McDermott said that scrap metal trading was regarded as a "high risk commodity in money laundering terms."

Ms McDermott said the FCA was "considering whether further regulatory action" was necessary against some of the banks it had studied, but did not comment on what specific sanctions it could impose. She said:

> "Banks and other financial organisations are in the front line regarding protecting against financial crime. We, and they, have a common interest in working in partnership to reduce the impact of financial crime both on the economy and more widely. Anti-money laundering measures and sanctions are

in place to protect us from criminal activity. Financial institutions need to take this responsibility seriously and we will do whatever is necessary to ensure they do."

The FCA, based in Canary Wharf, fined businesses a record £312m last year, more than triple its previous high of £89m. Among the largest fines were those against Barclays and Royal Bank of Scotland for their involvement in Libor-rigging.

The FCA also recently announced that it has fined Guaranty Trust Bank UK Ltd (GT Bank) £525,000 for failings in its anti-money laundering controls for high-risk customers. GT Bank, a subsidiary of Nigerian Guaranty Trust Bank PLC, started operations in London in May 2008, offering retail and wholesale banking products and services to private, corporate and institutional clients. The FCA said that between May 2008 and July 2010, GT Bank UK had failed to assess potential money-laundering risks, screen customers against sanction lists, establish the purpose of the accounts being opened in their London branch or review the activity of "high risk" accounts.

"Banks are at the front line in ensuring the proceeds of crime do not enter the UK financial system," said Tracey McDermott, the FCA's director of enforcement. She continued, "GT Bank's failures were serious and systemic and resulted in an unacceptable risk of handling the proceeds of crime."

London has been a favourite money-laundering venue for corrupt Nigerian politicians and criminal gangs. The role of British-based banks was highlighted during the trial and conviction of James Ibori, former governor of Nigeria's oil-producing Delta state, last year.

***

What is clear from the examples of sanctions that have been applied and background information from the FCA is that many international banks and financial institutions are not getting it right. To understand why this is the case I will look at the legal framework these businesses need to operate within and the technologies they can deploy to help them improve.

THE LEGAL FRAMEWORK

Large multinational banks and financial institutions have a plethora of legislation to comply with, including the USA Patriot Act, Money Laundering Regulations 2007, the Proceeds of Crime Act and the Criminal Justice Act.

This is often further compounded in Europe as legislation enacted via European Directives leaves member states to amend existing legislation or create new laws. We can see that member states have taken different approaches to the introduction of such EU law, with the UK taking a particularly *copper bottom* approach whilst other member states take a lighter touch approach.

There are also the international sanctions regimes to consider. Sanctions and embargoes are political trade tools, mainly put in place by the United Nations (UN) and the EU. The main aim of all UN sanctions and embargoes, as set out in the UN Charter, is to implement decisions by its Security Council to maintain or restore international peace and security.

The EU imposes sanctions and embargoes to further its Common Foreign and Security Policy (CFSP) objectives. It can impose measures to preserve peace and strengthen international security, promote international co-operation, and safeguard the common values and security of the EU. EU measures can also be imposed to uphold respect for human rights, democracy and the rule of law.

In addition to those of the UN and EU, sanctions and embargoes may be put in place by the Organisation for Security and Co-operation in Europe, which can also impose national arms embargoes.

POLITICALLY EXPOSED PERSONS

International banks and financial institutions then also need to consider Politically Exposed Persons (PEPs) in their policies and procedures. The term applies to persons who perform important public functions for a state. The definition used by regulators or in guidance is usually very general and leaves room for interpretation. For example the Swiss Federal Banking Commission in its guidelines on money laundering uses the term "person occupying an important public function", the US interagency guidance uses "senior foreign political figure" and the BIS paper *Customer due diligence for banks* defines it as "potentates".

The term should be understood to include persons whose current or former (up to one year after giving up any political function) position can attract publicity beyond the borders of the country concerned and whose financial circumstances may be the subject of additional public interest. In specific cases, local factors in the country concerned, such as the political and social environment, should be considered when deciding whether a person falls within the definition.

The following examples are intended to serve as aids to interpretation:

- Heads of state, government and cabinet ministers;
- Influential functionaries in nationalised industries and government administration;

- Senior judges;
- Senior party functionaries;
- Senior and/or influential officials, functionaries and military leaders and people with similar functions in international or supranational organisations;
- Members of ruling royal families;
- Senior and/or influential representatives of religious organisations (if these functions are connected with political, judicial, military or administrative responsibilities).

It is interesting to note that there has never been a published list of PEPs and so banks and financial institutions have to rely on third-party publishers to compile and manage these databases on their behalf.

THE CHALLENGE OF ENSURING COMPLIANCE

Certainly international financial institutions have an extremely difficult challenge in ensuring compliance. In the UK and many other jurisdictions they have developed a *risk-based approach* to anti-money laundering. This is a flawed approach as, having met literally hundreds of Money Laundering Reporting Officers (MLRO), I have seen that different people have differing views, thoughts and feelings on risk. Some have been highly risk adverse and at the other end of the scale there are also those who believe "It won't happen to us."

What is not in doubt is that a one-size-fits-all approach to compliance will not work, as often funds are transferred internationally through differing organisations and jurisdictions and as we have seen there are a wide range of different rules and regulations to comply with.

The nature and extent of systems and controls a financial institution will have to deploy will depend on a variety of factors, including:

- the nature, scale and complexity of the firm's business;
- the diversity of its operations, including geographical diversity;
- its customer, product and activity profile;
- its distribution channels;
- the volume and size of its transactions; and
- the degree of risk associated with each area of its operation.

How effective and efficient these systems and controls will be is often linked with the culture of the organisation and the investment these businesses make in people, infrastructure and technology. In some organisations compliance is seen by the board as a necessary evil and they invest as little as they can to maximise returns for the shareholders. What is clear is that technology can certainly be an effective enabler for financial institutions.

HOW TECHNOLOGY IS BEING DEPLOYED

Governments and financial institutions around the world need to work together to come up with creative measures to reduce money laundering, as technology is making it easier for persons to commit criminal acts. Improvements in information technology and other technological developments have made money laundering a big issue globally.

The internet in particular has made it a lot easier to do business, both legitimately and illegally. To make matters even more complex, the shift to online transactions has removed the confinement of jurisdiction. Today large amounts of money can be transferred from one country to another and back again in the time that it takes to click a few buttons.

Technology has made it easier to deregulate trade and allows for easier movement of assets across borders. But while the core objective of deregulation of trade is to promote economic growth, it has also made it easier for criminals to launder money.

In the past many financial firms have put together policies and procedures that created detection solutions and enterprise-wide programmes for financial crime and money laundering. These worked by establishing fixed rules based on monetary thresholds and detecting specific money laundering patterns and scenarios that breached these thresholds. As new money laundering methods were developed many of these systems were unable to uncover them, allowing the launderers new ways of hiding their criminal activity.

Today banks and financial institutions need to take their capabilities to the next level. The more forward-thinking institutions have developed technologies that monitor every transaction, enabling them to discover unusual types of behaviour and learn and adapt, comprehending new money laundering schemes as they arise.

The various elements that make up the risk to banks and financial institutions and the technology they use to detect these can be broken down into four main areas.

1. *Client risk* – often referred to as Know Your Client (KYC) or Customer Due Diligence (CCD). This is a two-part process that involves the client supplying information then the bank or financial institution verifying the information using documents, data or information from independent and reliable sources.

2. *Transactional risk detection* – identifying and filtering transactions that pose a greater risk of money laundering activity or identifying unusual transactions.

3. *Behaviour detection technology* – using specific technologies that are able to detect and draw attention to suspicious patterns of behaviour, which can often be hidden in large volumes of financial data.

4. *Reporting tools* – these alert compliance teams detailing the specific risks of any of the above.

Financial institutions that harness technology in these four areas will be able to analyse financial data and deter potential money launderers before they are able to proceed, providing the institution with protection in the form of full compliance with the regulations.

CLIENT RISK ASSESSMENT

Client risk assessment is one of the most important aspects in the prevention of money laundering and financial crime, as it is individuals who commit money laundering, often through a corporate veil. All financial firms need appropriate systems and controls for identifying and verifying their clients' identity, whether this is for individuals or corporate clients.

The verification of individuals can be undertaken using traditional documents such as passports and driving licences, or via electronic verification platforms. There are a number of drawbacks to using traditional documents, such as the ability to get forged documents. The quality of these can allow criminals and launderers to easily set up accounts.

Documents don't cover additional aspects of the money laundering regulations such as the requirement to check clients who are PEPs, or whether a client is on any of the sanctions lists. There are a number of electronic verification systems that can be used to verify identity without the use of documents or can use documents to verify additional aspects of the individual's identity, such as validating passports and driving licences. Electronic verification platforms can also carry out the necessary PEP and sanctions checks. Some systems such a SmartSearch can also monitor clients on an ongoing basis and create alerts for compliance teams when any warnings occur.

Business or corporate clients can require a much more complex process for financial institutions. For corporate clients the concept of beneficial owner comes into play; this is where any individual who owns or controls over 25% of an organisation has to be identified and depending on the risk-based assessment this also might require these individuals to be verified.

Often money launderers attempt to create legitimate businesses which are used to launder funds. A financial institution needs to understand the structure, ownership, control and purpose of the clients they take on. Some businesses will be incorporated, some may be unincorporated. Firms could also be dealing with trust or international client firms.

The verification of business clients involves confirming that the business exists and verifying individuals such as beneficial owners, directors and signatories. In the UK this can be done via Companies House, but again the requirement for screening against sanctions and PEPs will require additional technology.

Also, due to the Companies Act, more and more directors are registering themselves at the registered address of the business, so from a technology perspective the process can be cumbersome. There are however technology solutions that can streamline this process, as there is a dispensation under the Companies Act that allows Credit Referencing Agencies to hold directors' home address data for credit granting or for anti-money laundering. SmartSearch is such a platform, giving the ability to drill down to beneficial owners and directors, automate these checks in a single platform and undertake the appropriate sanction and PEP screening.

Financial institutions also need to screen business clients against sanctions and watch lists. There are a number of providers of such data, such as Dow Jones. Multinational financial firms can also utilise high-risk country alert flagging for further investigations for international transactions and overall transactional monitoring programmes.

TRANSACTION RISK DETECTION

Another key aspect to the prevention of money laundering is transaction monitoring; the ability to identify transactions that pose the greatest risk for money laundering activities. In the financial services sector this will vary from organisation to organisation, and depend on the complexity of the products, the size and the geographic spread. Transactions can fall into one of the three categories below.

1. **Fund related transactions** – Transactions that generate receipts into the firm or payments made by the firm could include transfers between accounts, rapid movements in or out of an account, or sudden activity through a previously dormant account.

2. **Transactional risk detection** – Behaviour where transaction values fall above specified limits and deviate from normal behaviour that can pose higher levels of suspicion is typically flagged for further investigation.

3. **Miscellaneous behaviour detection** – Frequent changes to an account can often be a signal that money laundering activity is being undertaken. This might be the settlement of accounts, movement of funds without the corresponding trade, or deposits of excess capital.

Financial institutions can use the KYC process to allocate clients into specific categories and then monitor activity. Take an example of a pizza restaurant which was set up to launder money. The restaurant seemed to have consistently high sales throughout the year with no lulls or exceptionally busy periods. By comparing the pizzeria's transactions against an industry peer group, the account suddenly appeared very suspicious. Similar pizza restaurants experienced a dip in sales just after the Christmas holiday, whereas the target restaurant did not have such a downturn. Using these profiling techniques coupled with transactional monitoring financial institutions can create a watching brief over their clients.

Transaction risk detection tools can then be combined with other techniques to enhance the ability to spot potential money laundering transactions. Behaviour detection, alerts and reporting tools provide regular checks and balances to ensure the transactional risk detection is constantly calibrated to ensure maximum efficiency and reduce the number of *false positives*:

- **Behaviour detection technology** – Many financial institutions are utilising Bayesian statistical algorithms with software to understand intentions and predict behaviour. These are used in combination with scenarios and patterns of behaviour that are of interest to the organisation, which can be a combination of rules and/or conditions which define the transaction pattern that is being detected. This could be a transfer of funds to or from a high-risk jurisdiction.

- **Alerts** – When a potential transactional or behavioural event is discovered this creates an alert, the function of this alert being to flag potential matches to fraud or money laundering teams which are then able to investigate. These alerts are manually reviewed together with the underlying data that created them. The results of these investigations could result in an alert being marked as a "false positive", escalating for further investigations, or making the necessary reports to the appropriate government body.

- **Reporting tools** – One of the key features of the adoption of technology processes for money laundering purposes is the use of reporting tools. All MLRO's of financial institutions are required to produce an annual report for the senior management team. Effective reporting systems are used to spot and deal with daily alerts, but can also be used to create monthly, quarterly or annual reports. One of the dangers of transactional and behavioural alerts is that they can create *false positives*. If these are not handled correctly then they can very easily and quickly overwhelm a financial institution. One example could be a mortgage; as this is an unusual size it could create an alert for an existing account, but it is quite legitimate and does not pose a risk.

SUMMARY

For financial institutions, compliance with the money laundering legislation means that they must adopt technology in some shape or form. Endeavouring to comply with the regulations would mean that these institutions would grind to a halt if they had to employ manual processes.

As we have seen, not all banks and financial institutions are getting this right; it is debatable if this is due to poor management or bad implementation of technology. There are now a number of second generation technologies which if implemented correctly can offer effective and efficient methods of ensuring compliance.

If we can be sure of one thing, it's that money laundering regulations are not going to disappear; if anything we will see more complex rules and regulations on an international scale. At the time of writing the 4th Money Laundering Directive is working its way through European Parliament, expected to be ratified later in 2013.

The current regulatory regime makes it a criminal offence for non-compliance and we can see from the heavy fines and reputational damage these firms have suffered that they could better protect themselves by the introduction of leading technology.

ETFS: WHAT IS THE PRICE OF ADMISSION?

BY DAYNA GOODWIN AND DR NOURIEL ROUBINI

ABOUT THE AUTHORS

Dayna Goodwin is a senior asset allocation strategist for Roubini Global Economics, focusing on developing forecasting models across asset classes. She holds a master's degree from New York University where she studied economics and financial risk management. She holds a bachelor's degree in economics and political science from Florida Atlantic University.

Dr Nouriel Roubini is the co-founder and chairman of Roubini Global Economics, an independent, global macroeconomic strategy research firm. The firm's website, Roubini.com, has been named one of the best economics web resources by *BusinessWeek*, *Forbes*, the *Wall Street Journal* and *The Economist*. He is also a professor of economics at New York University's Stern School of Business. Dr. Roubini has extensive policy experience as well as broad academic credentials. Dr. Roubini received an undergraduate degree at Bocconi University in Milan, Italy, and a doctorate in economics at Harvard University. Prior to joining Stern, he was on the faculty of Yale University's department of economics.

INTRODUCTION

EXCHANGE-TRADED FUNDS, or ETFs, emerged in the 1990s as a new type of investment fund which provides retail investors with the opportunity to diversify their holdings via exposure to indexes. Similar to mutual funds, which pool investor assets to transact in large shares on the primary market, ETFs present investors with a cost-efficient way to easily sell or purchase a basket of securities on exchanges. The ETF market has undergone rapid growth over the last two decades, in both market capitalisation, geographical and asset class coverage, and complexity relating to the construction.

Global ETF market capitalisation reached $1.76 trillion as of 31 December 2012, up nearly 30% from the previous year. The majority of this growth (roughly 18%) came from new cash inflows, led by the US ETF market which benefited from record inflows of $174 billion in 2012. The remaining growth in market capitalisation is attributed to asset price appreciation. The US closed 2012 with nearly 70% ($121 trillion) of the market as highlighted in Figure 1, with Europe ranking as the second largest market with 19% ($333 billion).

Figure 2 shows that equities lead the growth in all regional markets, with fixed income and commodities fund inflows ranking in second and third, respectively. Flow data suggests that part of the growth of US equity ETFs has been at the expense of traditional mutual funds, with the latter experiencing more than $400 billion in outflows since 2006, compared to inflows of $500 billion into equity ETFs over the same period.[1]

Figure 1 – the US dominates the global ETF market with nearly 70% of ETF assets

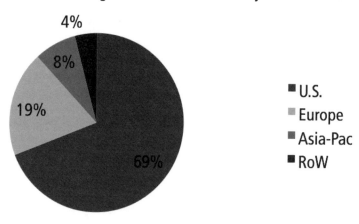

Source: Deutsche Bank

Figure 2 – annual cash inflows ($bn) by asset class

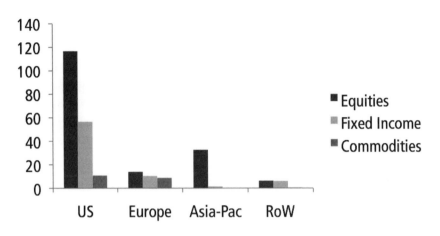

Source: Deutsche Bank

ETFS VS. MUTUAL FUNDS

Traditional mutual funds pool capital from many individual investors in a professionally-managed investment vehicle, providing retail investors with the opportunity to diversify their portfolios and participate in investments that may be restricted to smaller, individual investors. The majority of mutual funds are open-ended funds, meaning that fund shares can be bought from the mutual fund every day and that the mutual fund stands ready to repurchase shares from investors at the end of each business day at the net asset value (NAV). The mutual fund assets are managed by a qualified, regulated investment manager tasked with selling or buying securities to achieve the fund's stated investment objective. Such mutual funds are referred to as actively managed investment vehicles.

ETFs emerged as an alternative to actively managed mutual funds. Structured as open-ended mutual funds or unit investment trusts, the original ETFs replicated the underlying securities of broad US stock market indexes, such as the S&P 500. In other words, ETFs offer public investors the opportunity to pool their money to invest in a basket of securities and/or other assets in return for interest in the investment pool.

In contrast to the majority of mutual funds, ETFs are not actively managed, rather the ETF objective is to replicate the returns of the stated reference index; mutual funds that apply such a passive, low-turnover, low-cost strategy are known as index funds.

This passive investment strategy does not rely on the investment prowess of a portfolio manager, allowing ETFs to operate at a lower cost point and relieving investors of the need to evaluate fund manager performance when comparing available ETFs.

Another key difference between ETFs and mutual funds relates to how ETF shares are created and their availability to investors. The process of creating ETF shares for investors begins in the primary market where ETF sponsors sign participant agreements to designate financial institutions, typically large broker-dealers, as *authorised participants* (APs). APs have the exclusive right to purchase or redeem shares directly from the ETF and are only allowed to transact shares in blocks, typically 50,000 shares, referred to as *creation units*.

The purchase of creation units requires APs to assemble a predefined basket of securities and/or cash to be exchanged for the ETF shares. To redeem ETF shares APs deliver a block of ETF shares to the ETF sponsor and, in return, receive the designated basket of securities or the cash equivalent. After taking possession of the ETF shares, the authorised participant may sell the shares in the secondary market to market makers and retail or institutional investors. Figure 3 shows the structure of physical ETF replication.

ETF investors can only purchase and sell ETF shares in the secondary market, i.e. via exchanges, at market prices throughout the day, and may not sell shares or redeem shares directly from the ETF sponsor. The ability to trade intraday is ostensibly a benefit in terms of liquidity, but a drawback is that the transaction price may deviate from the true price of the underlying assets. This stands in contrast to mutual funds, which sell shares directly to, or redeem directly from, retail investors at the net asset value (NAV), which is usually calculated only once a day and verified by an independent third party.[2]

Figure 3 – process of creating ETF shares via physical replication

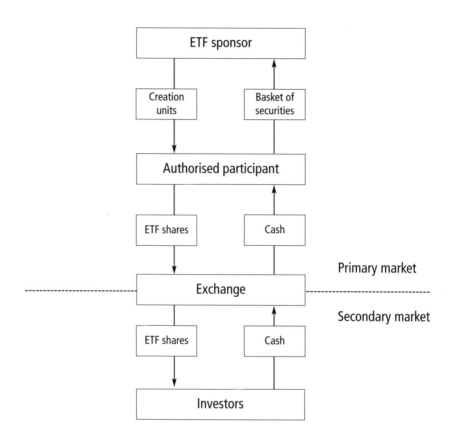

Source: Roubini Global Economics, BIS

THE ATTRACTION OF ETFS

ETFs have experienced strong global growth, cannibalising traditional investment vehicles such as mutual funds. There are three primary factors that drive the appeal of ETFs:

1. Cost efficiency and ease of execution
2. Access to a wide range of strategies
3. Liquidity.

1. COST EFFICIENCY AND EASE OF EXECUTION

From a cost perspective ETFs are relatively more attractive than direct investment in a wide portfolio of securities or mutual funds. As previously explained, ETFs allow investors to gain exposure to a basket of securities by investing in one investment vehicle. Directly assembling a basket of securities can be difficult for investors – particularly retail investors – as they face trading costs, and may face other restrictions when trying to assemble a comparable portfolio of assets.

As a simple illustration, imagine an investor wants to invest in the S&P 500. In order to replicate the S&P 500 returns s/he would have to purchase pro-rata shares of all 500 companies to accurately reflect the respective market capitalisations. Not only would this be time consuming, it may also be a cost prohibitive endeavour for investors (e.g. those who pay a fixed cost per trade). Conversely, investment funds benefit from economies of scale and so provide a relatively low cost and time efficient alternative to direct investment in assets.

It is important to ask whether traditional mutual funds or ETFs offer investors the most cost efficient solution to diversify investments. Generally, mutual funds and ETFs face similar costs, which include redemption fees, operational expenses and all asset-based costs incurred by the funds. However, mutual fund expense ratios (the percentage of assets paid to run the fund) are typically higher than those of ETFs due to larger operating costs, management fees to compensate for active fund management and load fees which are not part of the ETF cost structure.

Figure 4 summarises the divergence in ETFs and mutual funds across six fund types.[3] In addition to lower expense ratios, ETFs are generally able to reduce capital gains distributions rendering them more tax efficient. This continues to attract traditional as well as institutional investors and other sophisticated investors seeking to execute cost-friendly active trading strategies such as hedging.

Figure 4 – ETFs are a lower cost investment solution compared to traditional mutual funds

Average total operating expense		
Fund type	**Mutual funds**	**ETFs**
US Large-Cap Stock	1.31%	0.47%
US Mid-Cap Stock	1.45%	0.56%
US Small-Cap Stock	1.53%	0.52%
International Stock	1.57%	0.56%
Taxable Bond	1.07%	0.30%
Municipal Bond	1.06%	0.23%

Source: FINRA, Morningstar

2. ACCESS TO A WIDE-RANGE OF STRATEGIES

A second factor driving the popularity of ETFs is the increasingly wide variety of ETFs by asset class, geography and specialised risk-seeking strategies. ETFs began primarily as US-focused equity investments, but they have grown to include international, fixed income and commodity markets. Investors previously facing a dearth of low-cost investment vehicles now turn to ETFs for readily available, cost efficient access to various asset classes.

In addition to diverse asset classes, investors may also engage in short-term risk seeking trades through specialised strategy ETFs. Common examples of specialised strategy funds would be inverse or leveraged funds designed to achieve a short-term objective, rather than mirror long-term performance of the underlying index. Appealing to risk-seeking investors, these ETFs try to deliver the inverse return of a reference entity or return multiples of the reference index return, i.e. TZA Daily Small Cap Bear 3x Shares.

A caveat often overlooked by investors is that these specialised indexes are designed for extremely short time horizons and are typically reset every 24 hours. In other words, the objective of returning the multiple or inverse of the index is not evaluated over a long investment horizon. During periods of high volatility, severe underperformance of a 3x leveraged ETF relative to a leveraged index is guaranteed; this is a feature, rather than a bug, but this will not be understood by many less sophisticated investors until it is too late.

3. LIQUIDITY

Finally, ETFs share some of the convenient aspects of trading stocks, while the unique role of APs minimises liquidity constraints that these securities may encounter. Like stocks, ETFs can be purchased on a margin account, shorted and trade on exchanges throughout the day. However, stocks have a limited number of shares controlled by buyers and sellers on exchanges, yet the process of creating ETF shares makes it possible for APs to meet liquidity demand.

APs can satisfy demand for an ETF by creating more shares in the primary market and then selling them in the secondary market. The reverse also holds; if the supply of ETF shares outweighs demand APs can purchase shares in the secondary market for redemption in the primary market, thus maintaining the balance between supply and demand.

DEVIL IN THE DETAIL: THE DOWNSIDE OF ETFS

The exponential growth of the ETF markets relates to sheer market size as well as the increasing complexity of ETFs. ETF sponsors tout innovation as a means to reduce costs for investors, but at what price have these efficiency gains been achieved? The tangible efficiency gains (lower tracking error) reduce costs for ETF investors, but leave the investor and financial system vulnerable to intangible risks that arise from the increasingly complex, opaque and interconnected nature of ETFs.

SIMPLE IS BETTER: VANILLA REPLICATION

The rise in complexity primarily relates to the shift away from plain vanilla construction of ETFs to innovations relying on more exotic methods of replication, particularly synthetic replication. To clarify, let's begin with the plain vanilla approach to ETF replication.

Early on ETFs were assembled via a full physical replication strategy, which entails directly investing in the underlying assets, weighted to replicate the benchmark composition. In addition to being transparent, this approach to constructing the reference index is relatively cost efficient for deep, liquid markets. But as ETFs expand to cover broader markets and more illiquid assets APs are faced with wider bid-ask spreads when assembling the underlying basket, resulting in higher costs, particularly for high turnover funds. The cost of replication results in an ETF return below that of the reference index; this deviation from the performance of the reference index or securities is referred to as tracking error.[4]

TRACKING ERROR: PARTIAL REPRESENTATIVE REPLICATION

In effect, tracking error is a cost borne by investors in ETFs. Competing ETF sponsors, then, are motivated to circumvent these costs via alternative replication strategies to attract investors. One such strategy is a partial or representative replication strategy.

ETFs adopting a representative sampling strategy will invest in some, but not all, of the underlying securities that comprise the benchmark. This approach reduces costs by limiting the amount of securities in the underlying basket. However, holding a subset of the securities opens the door for divergences in ETF and benchmark performance, suggesting that tracking error is still a valid concern for the ETF investor. To offset divergent returns, ETF sponsors will often lend securities to earn additional returns.

The downside of this strategy is exposure to counterparty risk and possible liquidity risk. The first risk relates to the creditworthiness of the counterparty engaged in the lending activity, while the second risk could arise if the cash received in exchange for securities is invested in assets with limited liquidity. Given the lack of disclosure regarding the practice of utilising ETF underlying securities to engage in lending activities, investors will find it difficult to fully appreciate the associated risks.[5]

COUNTERPARTY AND LIQUIDITY RISK: SYNTHETIC REPLICATION

The ongoing quest to market the lowest-cost ETF possible led to another innovation in replication schemes, known as synthetic replication. This recent move toward the use of derivatives in lieu of holding the physical securities increases the complexity of ETFs and by virtue of the opaque nature of the swap market it further complicates the process of risk assessment – with particular regard to counterparty and liquidity risk.

Essentially, ETF sponsors market synthetic ETFs as having lower tracking error, but the nature of the replication strategy creates counterparty risk, a matter which is not marketed to potential investors. To have a clearer concept of the opaque and interconnected nature of synthetic ETFs we will go through a stylised example of a synthetic replication strategy.

Under a synthetic replication strategy, the APs present the ETF sponsor with cash for the creation units, rather than deliver a basket of the physical securities to the ETF. Separately, the ETF sponsor enters into derivatives contracts with a financial intermediary, usually an affiliated bank, to realise exposure to the reference assets. The financial intermediary receives cash equal to the notional exposure of the derivatives contract from the ETF sponsor and then posts a basket of collateral to the

ETF. The financial intermediary is now a counterparty that is required to deliver the returns of the reference index to the ETF.[6] This is illustrated in Figure 5.

Figure 5 – stylised example of a synthetic ETF and the counterparty exposure

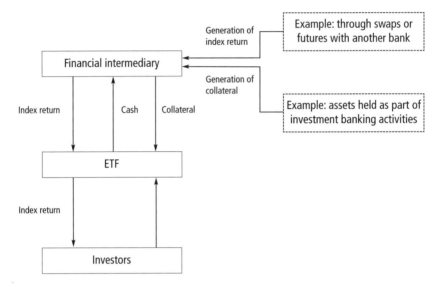

Source: Roubini Global Economics, BOE

LOWER TRADING COSTS VS. SYSTEMIC RISK

An interesting point that could exacerbate risks associated with synthetic replication is that banks are not required to post collateral that is related to the underlying reference index. Inasmuch, banks may find it advantageous to post illiquid collateral to the ETF, rather than fund these assets in unsecured or repo markets where they will be subject to greater haircuts to compensate for illiquidity. Ultimately, if the parent bank that acts as the ETF sponsor can exploit the lack of regulation regarding ETF collateral to reduce warehousing costs those savings can be passed on to the ETF, thus providing a more attractive cost structure to investors.

However, counterparties and ETFs are not required to consistently disclose detailed information pertaining to the quality of collateral or the nature of the derivatives transactions, thus the information available to market participants is opaque at best. While lower costs enhance the appeal of these ETFs, the lack of regulation regarding collateral posted to the ETF calls into question the ability of the ETF to weather a period of heightened concern for counterparty risk, such as we experienced during the 2008-09 Great Recession when there were major bank failures, including Lehman Brothers' disruptive bankruptcy.

In such a situation, the collateral mismatch (in other words, the collateral does not match the reference index) and illiquid nature of the posted collateral could galvanise investors to shed exposure to synthetic ETFs, in an effort to reduce counterparty risk. Under this scenario, both counterparty and funding liquidity risk can increase. In the wake of large ETF withdrawals and redemptions of ETF shares from APs trying to meet liquidity demands, banks may be forced to liquidate collateral assets posted to the ETF.

Moreover, such a scenario could also present funding liquidity risk to the counterparty institutions. Faced with significant ETF redemptions cash must be delivered against the illiquid collateral posted to the ETF, which could place a strain on the counterparty institution and reduce their ability to engage in market making. In both situations, these risks underscore the interconnectedness of the banking system and the ETF markets.[7]

CONCLUSION

In summation, the ETF market is a paradigm of financial innovation that has expanded the access to financial markets in an efficient, cost-effective manner, but not without introducing risks which may not yet be fully appreciated. By creating low-cost passive investment vehicles retail and larger institutional investors can execute efficient trades across asset classes, subsectors and regions to capture market beta, without paying for ephemeral alpha generation via traditional funds. Certainly, ETF growth reflects the demand for alternatives to traditional investment schemes, but with the rising sophistication of ETFs the risks have also expanded.

The chief risks we outlined stem from the innovation of synthetic replication, which has greatly expanded the complex and opaque nature of these financial instruments. In doing so, it becomes increasingly difficult for market participants to properly assess the different layers of risk. The use of derivatives contracts increases the counterparty exposure between parties, resulting in an interconnectedness that could pose greater risks than anticipated. Although global banks are not ETF investors their role as securities lenders, counterparties and market makers reinforces the link between the ETF market and banking system.

While these factors do not definitely point to systemic risk, the lack of clarity surrounding the distribution and depth of risks, and the interconnected nature of these markets, does create potential for systemic risk under extreme circumstances.

ENDNOTES

[1] '2012 ETF Review and 2013 Outlook', Deutsche Bank Markets Research (11 January 2013).

[2] 'What You Should Know About Exchange Traded Funds', NYSE Regulation (2009).

[3] FINRA, Morningstar.

[4] 'BIS Working Papers No 343: Market Structures and systemic risks of exchange traded funds', Bank of International Settlements (April 2011).

[5] 'Financial Stability Report Issue No. 29', Bank of England (June 2011).

[6] Bank of International Settlements, Bank of England.

[7] Bank of International Settlements.

ONLINE DOCUMENT STORAGE AND DELIVERY SERVICES: THE FINANCIAL SERVICES CONTEXT

BY BEN MARTIN

ABOUT THE AUTHOR

Ben Martin is a founder and director of Safe4 Information Management Limited, a UK business that offers a highly secure locally-hosted online service for the delivery and storage of documents on behalf of customers in a range of different business sectors.

www.safe-4.co.uk

INTRODUCTION

IN 2013 THE majority of people expect to use online services to manage most aspects of their lives. This extends from doing the weekly shopping, planning and booking holidays, buying cinema and theatre tickets, to a wide range of other everyday activities. For many years financial services providers have recognised this, and have been making bank and credit card statements available electronically, and providing a range of other internet-based services to their online customers.

But could the financial services provider be doing more? Could they be helping their clients to manage their lives electronically in other ways?

THE DEMOGRAPHICS ARE CHANGING

The generation of people that has emerged from schools and universities in the last couple of decades is already accustomed to managing their affairs online. Familiarity with the use of internet-based services is strongly established with the younger generations, and though there will be for some time a core segment of the population who are uncomfortable with computers and who distrust web-based services, such inhibitions are becoming less of an issue to service providers.

On a corporate level, including many examples in the legal sector and among independent financial advisors, senior management are often reticent about using online services to support their private clients. Traditional ways of doing business still prevail in many cases, largely because a small rump of long-established clients may not have a computer at home and they may prefer everything delivered on paper.

While the wishes of such clients must be respected, this causes visible frustration among the younger members of such firms who have been using their laptops or smart phones to handle information and documents for years, and who realise that a growing majority of the wider population want to be serviced in this way.

THE START OF A DIFFERENT TYPE OF CLIENT RELATIONSHIP?

Of course, there has been some inception of online technology into business. Financial service providers are already using online services as a means of delivering information. This often takes the form of documents such as statements, and contracts of one form or another. Handling routine financial transactions on behalf of clients is of course a two-way activity involving very secure data management services, often accessing online databases in real time to establish balances, make payments and a host of other activities. But what about documents in a wider context? A large number of transaction types still require the physical transfer of hard copy documents, even though electronic lodgement of these documents in a secure vault would save everyone time and money.

There is also the option that the financial service provider could make such secure facilities available to their clients even when they are not executing one of their own transactions. Why shouldn't the client be able to store other critical information in such a vault, subject to appropriate restrictions on volumes and content type? This could create a different link with the client, perhaps generating new levels of trust and confidence in the service provider, particularly if the document vault were to carry the service provider's branding and other messaging to reinforce their proposition.

The answer to the questions I have posed is that there are already independent internet-based document delivery and storage service providers active in the UK who can make such facilities available today, at minimal cost, on behalf of the financial services business.

WHAT ABOUT SECURITY?

Any service that offers a document storage facility on behalf of a client must be as secure as today's technologies will allow. The client must have complete confidence that any documents they place in an online vault will be unavailable to anybody other than users who have been specifically authorised to access the information that the vault contains.

Most large financial service providers, such as banks and building societies, have already invested considerable sums in making their online systems as secure as possible. The smaller providers, however, may not have the resources to implement such systems themselves and may find that specialist third-party organisations are better placed to offer these facilities reliably and cost-effectively, and with robust, secure architectures.

The reputable and successful providers of secure internet-based document services all utilise encrypted connections to the internet. This follows the same approach used by banks and other large financial service businesses and means that the link to the internet cannot be intercepted or accessed fraudulently.

THE CLOUD

There has been much comment on the use of the cloud as an option for information storage, much of it from parties who do not possess the knowledge or experience to influence the views of others. Senior members of businesses that provide financial services have frequently expressed negative views of the cloud without necessarily appreciating what is involved. The cloud is in fact a means of storing information on a series of very powerful servers that are hosted and managed by third-party organisations, in an environment described as multi-tenanted.

Some very reputable organisations offer cloud-based storage facilities and provide a package of services that manage their customers' data to the highest standards available. Such services include an array of backup and fault-tolerant hardware and software infrastructure that can guarantee 99.99% uptime.

Cloud storage services are widely used by banks and even governments as overflow or emergency facilities to supplement their own internal environments. This is not generally publicised, but the leading cloud storage providers also maintain a regime of firewall protection measures that significantly reduce the risk of intruder access when compared with many corporate organisations.

My view is that cloud-based storage is likely to be better managed, more resilient and more secure than storage services provided by most corporates. A further major advantage is that by using an external cloud-based document service, the service provider does not need to open up their own IT environment or domain to external users. This brings a considerable reduction in risk as well as a financial saving in management and oversight.

WHERE IS CLOUD DATA STORED?

Rightly, many organisations are very concerned about where their data is being stored. This concern arises largely from issues relating to international legal jurisdictions and the intrusive rights claimed by some governments to interrogate data that passes through their jurisdiction. For this reason organisations such as Safe4 Information Management use cloud storage facilities in the UK only, thus eliminating any issues relating to potential contravention of safe harbour and data protection regulations.

In the case of Safe4 Information Management, and potentially with other UK businesses, the advantage of operating under English law can also be significant. In recent times, there have been many instances of contractual breaches by large high-profile internet-based companies who host their data in many different parts of the globe, often being dealt with under the laws of California – a daunting prospect indeed for a small or medium-sized UK practitioner should problems arise.

WHAT TYPES OF SERVICE PROVIDER ARE USING THE CLOUD?

I have made mention of the different types of relationship that can be offered to a client by the service provider allowing their online storage facilities to be used by their clients to hold personal documents. When coupled with the additional option of utilising cloud-based resources, a compelling proposition can be developed: give the client access to a secure vault that can be used to hold their personal documents, thus binding them closer through a stronger relationship, and deliver the service by using a specialist, high quality, third-party provider that removes the need for costly investment in the procurement and management of a complex IT infrastructure.

A number of different organisations are starting to realise the potential for this proposition. Some simple illustrations of these are:

- *Banks* – although most large banks use their own IT infrastructure to manage all of their online client services, several are starting to realise that not everything has to be handled by their own internal IT department. For example, one of the leading banks in South Africa has plans to offer their online customers an internet-based service to hold their own personal documents, subject to reasonable use restrictions.

- *Independent financial advisors (IFAs)* – in the UK, recent regulation has had a profound impact on the IFA sector, with many small firms exiting the market and large-scale consolidation. IFAs have traditionally provided their clients with large volumes of information, usually in paper format, thus giving the client a file management problem of their own. Namely, what actually needs to be kept, and for how long? For the client that needs to travel frequently, the ability to gain access to information online from anywhere at any time is compelling and can bring a significant competitive advantage to the IFA. Regulatory compliance will also be improved if an online service with a clear audit trail of document delivery and access is used.

- *Syndicated bank lending* – smaller banks that offer lending services on a syndicated basis through a managing agent can gain enormous benefits by providing a cost-effective means of delivering and gathering information relating to a loan deal. There are several very large and costly services widely used by the bigger banks to handle syndicated lending, but the cost and complexity of these systems is not necessarily appropriate for the mid-tier or smaller bank.

- *Mortgage consultants and brokers* – property transactions involve significant volumes of documentation and frequently the transaction is delayed while this information is being moved between the parties in paper form. An online vault service will dramatically reduce the delays caused by waiting for paper documents to arrive.

- *Private banking and wealth management* – similar to the IFA sector, private banking and wealth management involves large volumes of documentary information and often access to this can be difficult for the client whilst travelling or away from their home or normal place of business. The simplicity and immediacy of a secure online document vault will greatly enhance client service, and will provide all parties with a clear record of delivery and usage of documents.

- *Pension providers* – most pension fund operators make their online databases accessible to their clients or the client's IFA. This provides up-to-the-minute information on valuations and the performance of investments. However, the documents generated by such systems are usually presented to the client in paper form, often to maintain an audit trail and evidence of delivery by the IFA. Frequently documents are sent in PDF format as email attachments; as suggested below, this is not necessarily a satisfactory way of achieving the delivery objective. An online document vault service will give better protection and security for all parties by recording not only when documents are delivered, but also when they have been opened.

- *Insurers and brokers* – it is possible to complete the process of setting up many types of insurance online, with policy documents and terms of business being delivered in PDF form for the client to store electronically. This is highly convenient for travel insurance, for example. However, much commercial insurance requires not only extensive documentary records during the proposal process, but rigorous management of documents as evidence of compliance. This is particularly true in the case of specific types of insurance, such as Professional Liability, which has become prohibitively expensive for practitioners such as tax advisors, accountants, IFAs and property surveyors and valuers.

- *Identity verification* – proof of identity and residence is a mandatory requirement before many types of transaction can be undertaken. In some situations it is necessary to perform such checks more than once, and thus access to online storage can be a huge benefit to both the service provider and their client to avoid the need for multiple copies of documents to be captured and stored. Anti-money laundering checking is a highly sophisticated and automated process, and does not generate any documents that require storage. However, compliance checks such as the normal *fact find* and *know your client* routines do generate a requirement for document storage. It is advantageous for both provider and client to have access to these documents, thus maintaining regulatory compliance and offering a transparent service to the client.

- *Employee vetting* – in the increasingly-regulated world of financial services it is frequently necessary for extensive checks to be carried out on potential employees before they are engaged. Often Criminal Records Bureau checks are needed for certain posts and evidence of qualifications is now becoming mandatory in some environments. These document records can be shared by employer and employee in such a way that the employee can retain access to the information when they move to new employment by using a secure online document service.

- *Trust and estate planning practitioners* – the business of writing wills and advising on inheritance and estate planning is often carried out by specialist lawyers or other dedicated practitioners. However, a number of banks and their subsidiaries do offer such services and IFAs are frequently involved in estate planning activities. The concept of placing a testator's will in a secure vault on their behalf, along with the other documents that will be essential while performing the probate process, makes the gathering of information very rapid and simple at a time when those involved are bereaved and facing a difficult period. If, for example, the testator were to place an asset and liability register in the vault, with records of passwords and other access requirements, this could be maintained as circumstances change and made available to the executors of the estate immediately after death, thus simplifying and shortening the probate process. It is also very easy for the testator to share their will with the beneficiaries and executors before death using an online service.

THE BUSINESS CASE

Even if there are significant benefits to be gained by the service provider through the use of a secure online document delivery and storage service, most organisations will only choose to do so if there is a clear financial advantage. It must save money.

The most obvious savings to be had are in the reduced use of consumables associated with delivering physical documents: paper, envelopes, printer toner and, most obviously, postage. The more efficient use of staff time is a major factor – it is much quicker and easier to place an electronic file into a document vault, knowing that the client will be notified automatically of its delivery, than it is to print and post the document and file an internal copy. And if the client loses or misfiles the paper document and requests a copy, the whole process must be carried out again.

However, the biggest savings are to be gained when the documents that are generated during the execution of normal business processes are placed programmatically into the vault on behalf of the client, using an application programming interface. Such processes require no staff intervention at all. Optimising the business process to achieve maximum efficiency will allow the service provider to obtain clear and significant financial benefits, in addition to the softer advantages of enhancing client service and strengthening the client relationship.

WHAT ABOUT COMPLIANCE?

Today's financial services industry is more closely regulated than ever and if anything will become even more so in time. Achieving and maintaining compliance are potentially onerous tasks for the smaller practitioner and even for large organisations can be costly and difficult.

Providing evidence of compliance in a paper-based environment can be a challenge. Maintaining an accurate internal filing system is obviously good practice and virtually all organisations would see this as an essential business activity. However, this does not deal with what the client actually received from the provider and what was then done with the information thereafter.

As mentioned above, the service provided by systems such as Safe4 covers these issues without any effort on the part of the financial service provider. A full and clear audit trail is maintained, showing an unequivocal record of the precise date and time of delivery and any subsequent actions performed by either client or provider. Not only can the provider offer evidence that a document was delivered, but also that the client accessed it at a specific time.

Sometimes it is helpful to know that the client has not opened a document – inbuilt reporting systems make such information available very easily. In effect, by doing the client's filing for them as an automatic consequence of doing their own filing, the service provider extends good information management practice into the client domain. No more lost or misplaced documents – a valuable benefit indeed for the client.

Compliance with the requirements of a professional indemnity insurance policy can also be demonstrated; in some environments that require accurate records to be captured as a service is carried out – for example a property survey or valuation – evidence of good practice or otherwise is easily obtained.

DOCUMENT DELIVERY

EMAIL IS NOT AN EFFECTIVE MEANS OF DELIVERING DOCUMENTS

It is surprising how many small-to-medium financial and legal service practitioners are reliant on email as a means of achieving document delivery to their clients. While this may offer some superficial advantage, it is fraught with risk. In essence, the provider simply sends the document as an attachment and hopes for the best. Even if read-receipts are used, there is no evidence that an attachment was ever received or opened.

There have been countless cases of emails containing very sensitive attachments being forwarded in error, with very costly consequences. Encrypted email has not brought a satisfactory solution. If the client wishes to access confidential information while away from their own computer, this can often be difficult and sometimes impossible to achieve.

THE FUTURE OF DOCUMENT DELIVERY

Decisions as to how to handle client document delivery will naturally focus primarily on the key issue of cost. Based solely on this criterion, the use of a secure cloud-based service offered by an external provider brings clear and obvious benefits. No capital investment, no complex IT hardware or software to manage, no costs of any kind other than those reflecting the actual usage of the service. And measurable savings every time a document is delivered.

But perhaps the greater benefit is to be achieved in the so-called softer sense, by engendering a closer relationship with the client and making it easier to hang on to them. It is widely recognised that it costs about ten times as much to find and win a new client as it does to retain an existing one. Implementing the use of a secure document delivery and storage service can be an excellent tool in maintaining a client relationship, particularly if the service provider allows the client to upload and hold their own information in the vault.

* * *

Employing online storage and delivery of documents and information creates the prospect for firms to save money, improve service and retain clients more easily. In today's challenging economic environment, these can only be valuable outcomes for the financial service provider.

SENTIMENT TRADING – PARADIGM-SHIFT FOR INTRADAY TRADERS

BY STEFAN NANN AND JONAS KRAUSS

ABOUT THE AUTHORS

Stefan Nann is co-founder and joint CEO of social media analytics company Stockpulse GmbH, which provides trading signals calculated from social media talk. He holds a diploma degree in Information and Decision Systems from the University of Cologne. As part of his current PhD program at the University of Cologne, he attended an 18-month research period at Massachusetts Institute of Technology (MIT). His work mainly focuses on prediction of stock market movements based on public data, analysis of social network structures and collective intelligence in social media. His research has been published at numerous conferences, and in books and journals. Before Stefan Nann founded Stockpulse he worked for three years at a social media monitoring company in Switzerland. He further gained practical experience in project management and software development in the USA and Switzerland.

Jonas Krauss is co-founder and joint CEO of the company StockPulse GmbH. His work is mainly concerned with predictive analytics on big data and system development. Before his current position he worked for three years at a company specialising in social media monitoring in Switzerland and the USA. He studied Business Information Systems at the University of Cologne and the Hawaii Pacific University. After achieving his diploma degree he continued his academic curriculum at the Massachusetts Institute of Technology (MIT) as a visiting student and at the University of Cologne as a doctoral candidate. His research has been published at a variety of renowned conferences and covers trend predictions through analysing web communication and sentiment analysis.

INTRODUCTION

SENTIMENT TRADING IS currently developing into one of the largest trends in trading strategies. Today's computing power allows one to handle the large data flood streaming in from digital social media sources. Data from these sources (e.g. Twitter) bears valuable information and can generate alpha – if it is structured and aggregated in meaningful ways.

In this article we give an overview of the methodologies used to detect sentiment in social media and news sources, explain how to derive trading signals from these data, and demonstrate how to use these signals for successful trades.

DETECTING SENTIMENT IN COMMUNICATION

[Excerpt from Nann, Krauss and Schoder, 2013]

This section is an excerpt from an academic paper that was published in May 2013. In this paper we demonstrated how sentiment data could be applied to implement a simple trading strategy for stocks from the S&P 500 Index. Over a period of six months from June 2011 to November 2011, we calculated up to ten buy and sell signals on each trading day, based on sentiment data collected from social media and news sources.

We then analysed how a trading strategy based on these signals would have performed depending on assumed transaction costs (mainly hypothetical commission fees and spread). When assuming an average cost of 20bp per transaction, our virtual trading strategy showed a performance of ~72% while the S&P 500 slightly decreased in value. The following paragraphs are taken from the chapter describing the method for sentiment retrieval in communication.

For this paper, we collected 2,971,381 messages concerned with stocks of the S&P 500 Index during a six-month period from 1 June to 30 November. The first step is to assign these messages to stocks. For that we filtered the dataset by either looking for messages in sub-forums concerned with particular stocks on online message boards or by using Twitter's *cash tag*. The cash tag is a stock's ticker symbol with a preceding dollar sign ($). Not considering spam at this point (there are more details on how we filter spam in the following paragraphs) we can rely on the fact that a tweet which contains a cash tag refers to the stock price or something related to the financial value of the underlying company (e.g. where we find the cash tag $MSFT we assume this is a tweet relating to the company Microsoft).

For sources other than Twitter, stock specific communication can be accessed in sub-forums which exist for each component of the S&P 500. In these sub-forums users exclusively discuss topics related to a particular company. For example Yahoo! Finance provides direct access to a stock's sub-forum by appending the ticker symbol to the following hyper-reference: finance.yahoo.com/mb (so for instance, this would give finance.yahoo.com/mb/MSFT for company Microsoft). With this method, each tweet and forum post can clearly be assigned to a single company, which is important to ensure only relevant communication is considered when calculating sentiment.

Thus we get a relatively precise assignment of messages relating to a specific company or stock, which helped us to avoid some common name entity conflicts (as mentioned in Yerva, Miklós and Aberer (2010)). Although we cannot rely on the fact with full certainty, we can assume that people talk about companies or company-related issues when posting in the financial discussion board for Apple, rather than about the fruit. Nevertheless, after collecting all messages we applied a spam filter which cleaned our data set. Our self-developed spam filter searched, for example, for posts which intended to insult other users without contributing relevant information. Most of these posts can be identified by the usage of scurrile and nasty language. Everything of this sort was removed from the data set.

The next step was to apply sentiment analysis to microblog messages, forum posts and traditional news using a naïve Bayes classifier with an adapted bag-of-words in combination with part-of-speech tagging to find negations and filter spam based on keywords. The basis of the applied sentiment methodology can be found in Krauss, Nann and Schoder (2012). One of our key findings is that the quality of sentiment recognition depends on how specifically the sentiment analysis algorithms are adjusted to the analysed context. The more context-specific the algorithms are designed the higher the quality of sentiment recognition will be. This is determined for example by the choice of bag-of-words and the adjustment of part-of-speech tagging. For example, authors use different language and words to write a positive review about a digital camera than they would when saying something positive about their favourite stock. We adjusted the sentiment analysis very specifically to the stock market domain.

For this reason we initially read a few hundred tweets and posts from the available dataset and manually annotated these with positive or negative sentiment. This sample data was used to train our self-developed sentiment algorithm. In the next step we applied the trained algorithm to a newly and not annotated data sample from the available data set to determine the precision of the sentiment algorithm. Also, in a manual process we defined lists of positive (e.g. buy, long, call, etc.) and negative (e.g. sell, short, put, etc.) words which resulted in our bag-of-words. During text analysis the algorithm scans the content for these words.

We also manually defined specific words for part-of-speech tagging. The word 'don't', for example, will be used during part-of-speech-tagging, if a user posts "I don't sell my shares", this will be recognised and labelled with positive sentiment since the key word 'don't' will give the negative key word 'sell' the opposite meaning.

At the end of the process, the algorithm calculated a ratio (decimal number) based on the occurrences of positive and negative labels in a tweet or post. The sum of all ratios for all messages of a specific stock represents the aggregated sentiment value which was used to predict the daily stock price.

Messages from all sources were considered with equal weight in our model. It is obvious that different data sources contain different value contributions. Tweets will probably have a lower half-life than traditional news, which usually references a longer time period. It is the subject of further research to design a process which evaluates these aspects of every single source separately.

As not all stocks from the S&P 500 receive equal attention in social media, there are substantial differences in the average number of messages written each day for different stocks. For instance, Apple Inc. is one of the most discussed equities on the web and many more messages are posted for Apple Inc. than for other index components. Thus we require an adjustment of sentiment values based on the average number of messages. For this work we chose the simple moving average (SMA) to achieve comparability for equities of differing attention levels. Sentiment values were used as a stock price movement predictor, with positive values indicating an upward movement and negative values indicating a downward movement.

We began calculating our predictor one month after commencing data collection because we used a 30-day simple moving average (SMA30) to calculate sentiment values. Thus, predictions of stock price movements were made each trading day from 1 June to 30 November 2011. For each trading day, t, the predictor considered sums of positive and negative messages for each stock on the S&P 500 and weighted them based on the SMA30.

This value was used to predict stock price change on day $t + 1$, predicting an increase in the case of positive values and a decrease in the case of negative values. Sentiment values can assume any value larger or smaller than zero.

Sentiment trading = No. of positive messagesSMA30 of positive messages − No. of negative messagesSMA30 of negative messages

Through weighting current messages in relation to the SMA30, it is possible to compare stocks that have significantly different attention levels and thus strongly differing message averages. We chose a 30-day average because it takes into account enough days to even out positive and negative peaks in communication without being too static in comparison to longer periods. Longer periods would carry the danger of ignoring short-term anomalies in communication – e.g. in the case of earnings releases or bankruptcies – which often lead to a strong increase in message numbers.

Let us quickly recapitulate here what has been done so far. First, we filtered communication from a variety of sources ranging from social media channels like Twitter or Yahoo! Finance message boards to classic news media to identify which companies are the subject of interest in each message. Second, we used textual processing and a naïve Bayes classifier to detect the general mood in each message. Third, by aggregating mood values for each stock on each trading day, we were able to calculate a numerical value representing the sentiment for the stocks. The result is data in the form of a time series for each of the 500 components from the S&P 500. The next step is to derive trading signals from these data, which is described in the following section.

DERIVING TRADING SIGNALS FROM SENTIMENT DATA

[Excerpt from Nann, Krauss and Schoder, 2013]

This section continues with citing the chapter where we describe the derivation of trading signals from the previously calculated sentiment time series. A signal generally looks like this: positive sentiment values (greater than zero) predict a stock price increase (open to close) on the upcoming trading day; vice versa for negative sentiment values.

Each trading day, we determined the level of sentiment (threshold) for each stock where the historical ratio of correct to total predictions was maximised. Sentiment values count as prediction signals only if the absolute sentiment value lies above the threshold. For instance, for a threshold of two, a sentiment value of one would not be considered a signal to trade. We systematically determined historic prediction ratios by conducting a sensitivity analysis of sentiment thresholds each trading day for each stock.

This was done by looking at all past trading days, comparing the sentiment on day t with the stock price change on day t + 1, summing dates on which a positive/negative sentiment on day t corresponded with a positive/negative stock price change on day t +1, and finally building the ratio for each threshold.

Results were statistically significant on a level of 0.05 (right-sided significance test). On average, we obtained ten stocks per trading day that had statistically significant prediction ratios greater than 0.5. We further found that a look ahead of one day delivered the best results, which means that sentiment values of day t predicted stock price changes of day t + 1 with the highest accuracy compared to predictions for day t + 2 or day t + 3.

sum correct predictions (sentiment threshold)-total predictions (sentiment threshold). →max

Our results show that publicly available data in microblogs, forums and news on day t has predictive power for stock price changes on day t + 1. Table 1 displays the overall prediction performance and the performance for each month.

Table 1 – prediction ratios

Predictions	All	Ratio buy predictions	Ratio sell predictions
Entire period	60.38%	60.69%	60.03%
November 2011	57.54%	60.71%	54.74%
October 2011	63.76%	63.16%	64.81%
September 2011	52.63%	48.98%	55.86%
August 2011	67.34%	67.52%	67.18%
July 2011	60.99%	63.38%	56.79%
June 2011	59.73%	59.01%	60.61%

The percentage values display the ratios of correct predictions for all analysed stocks over the entire period from 1 June to 30 November 2011. For example, 60.38% means that ~60% of all stocks for which sentiment had significant prediction ratios in the past delivered correct predictions in the period considered. In sum, the algorithm made 1300 predictions over the entire period (126 trading days). Table 1 lists predictions for rising stock prices through positive sentiment and predictions of falling stock prices through negative sentiment. Both cases do not differ significantly.

Again, let us quickly summarise what we have described in this section so far. By systematically comparing our buy and sell signals with actual stock price changes we found that roughly 60% of all signals were correct. Approximately ten signals were calculated each trading day which means that trading these signals manually would have been difficult in the real world. Anyway, we briefly illustrate the results from the virtual trading based on these signals in Figure 1.

Figure 1 – comparison of cumulative returns on investments for our trading model and the SPY certificate from June 1 to November 30 (without transaction cost)

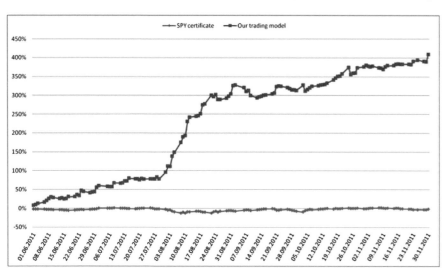

Source: Nann, Krauss and Schoder (2013)

In the paper we continued to analyse how a simple trading strategy based on these signals would have performed by looking at daily stock prices. However, for this article we would like to go further and provide detailed examples of conducting successful intraday trades based on sentiment signals. We do so by looking at intraday stock price developments – for example signals taken from the system StockPulse (www.stockpulse.de), which is a company providing sentiment data and signals for traders and investors.

SENTIMENT TRADING: EXAMPLES

ONE DAY, TWO TRADES – DRILLISCH AND TUI ON 17 JULY 2013

The two trade signals for Drillisch (bullish/long) and Tui (bearish/short) in the Daily Sentiment Trader[1] from 17 July 2013 were both confirmed later that day. At first, the share of Drillisch hesitated to develop a clear upward movement right after market-opening, but then rose until market-closing and closed clearly positive.

The forecast of +0.62%, which was generated automatically by Pulse Picks[2], was reached at noon on that day for the first time. The stock had its intraday high between 3pm and 4pm and was able to maintain this level, with a short interruption, for more than an hour (Figure 2).

Figure 2 – intraday chart for the Drillisch-share; it rose almost continuously after a non-uniform start

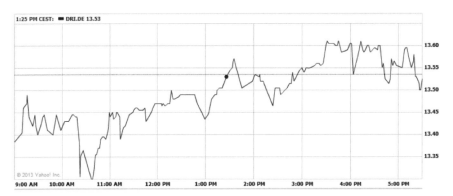

The bearish signal for Tui was realised in an even shorter space of time. Right after market-opening the share started rising, but only until approximately 9:20am. From this time on the predicted downward movement took place. Between 11am and 12:30pm the share moved to its intraday low of -1.32%, which comfortably exceeded the Pulse Picks forecast of -0.82%.

Figure 3 – intraday chart for the Tui-share; shortly after 11am the stock had already lost much more than predicted

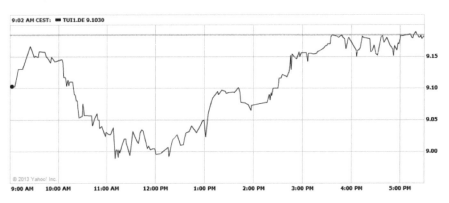

Both cases show that signals from social media and news sentiment are short-term intraday signals. Thus, a trader's stop strategy should tolerate short developments against the predicted performance. After market open Drillisch shares rose first but then slumped into negative briefly to about 0.6% (compared to the opening price). Although the stock price recovered quickly, traders with a conservative stop-loss would possibly have exited already between 10am and 11am when the drop happened. A solid stop strategy allowing for temporary drops was thus required to successfully trade this signal.

The same pattern could be observed for the TUI signal. The share price first went in the opposite direction to the signal. But then, between 10am and 11am, the stock price fell significantly and this trend even continued until after 11am. Then, in the following longer sideways phase, the price fluctuated below the predicted value – there was more than enough time for intraday traders to realise profits from their short position.

PULSE PICK BEARISH FOR K+S – AN EXCEPTIONAL TRADING OPPORTUNITY

It is a very rare event when a DAX30 stock loses a quarter of its value in just half a day – 30 July 2013 was one of those days. The shares of fertiliser manufacturer K+S lost up to 27% of their value at their lowest point that day, after the Russian competitor Urakali annulled an important trade consortium and warned against falling fertiliser prices. In consequence, share prices of the entire industry were sent into a tailspin.

Before market open, and therefore before the landslide losses, the automatic sentiment analysis of StockPulse generated a bearish signal for K+S shares. In fact the signal was calculated before 8am in the morning, giving enough time to place orders if a trader's assessment was consistent with the StockPulse trend prediction.

The stock had lost significantly in pre-market trading. Yet, in spite of these losses, the share price plummeted again at 8:30am (Figure 4). This shows that in many cases sentiment signals from social media and/or news should be understood as ultra-short-term indicators, meaning that predicted price targets are often reached within a few hours in the case of a true signal, or even faster.

Figure 4 – chart of K+S from 30 July 2013; even before the beginning of pre-market at Lang & Schwarz the StockPulse system recognised a bearish signal

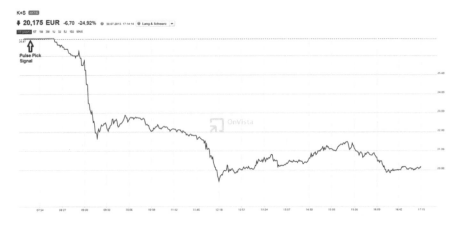

KEEP AN EYE ON THE MARKET – E.ON, RWE AND INFINEON

An example which shows that signals from social media sentiment can function even in an uncertain market environment comes from 6 August 2013. While the outlook for German indices was unclear according to social media sentiment, the *Daily Sentiment Trader* newsletter reported clear trading forecasts, including for E.ON, RWE and Infineon. The system produced a bearish signal for the two energy groups while it generated an opposite bullish signal for the technology group.

Figure 5 – charts from 6 August 2013 by comparison: The DAX (left) significantly dropped after 3:30pm; Infineon (2nd from left) showed a significant increase up to that point and only went down together with the DAX drop; the energy stocks RWE (3rd from left) and E.ON (right) clearly dropped in the morning and slipped further into red in parallel with the falling index

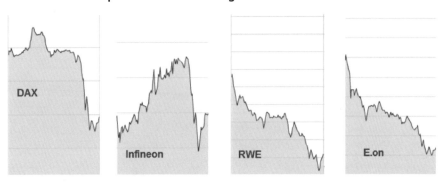

Source: Authors' illustration

This day (Figure 5) showed how important it is for traders to have an eye on the market in addition to their own positions. Initially, all three shares moved in the predicted direction. While shares of RWE and E.ON significantly declined after market opening in Frankfurt, shares of Infineon moved up after a very brief turn into negative.

It gets interesting when we have a look at the progress of the overall market. The German main index DAX stayed, apart from a brief high, in a very narrow range around 8400 points until the opening of US markets at 3:30pm. The DAX then turned negative and lost more than 100 points till 4:40pm. In consequence, the value of the three stocks fell together with the market.

In this market phase it made sense for traders to close a possible long position in Infineon, taking accrued profits. At the same time, the falling overall market indicated that it might be worthwhile to continue to hold short positions. A trader who did this with E.on and RWE would have benefited from the continuous downward movement after the beginning of US market hours.

SENTIMENT TRADING: NOT JUST A PARADIGM-SHIFT FOR TRADERS

The examples from the last section show how beneficial it can be to use sentiment data from social media and news for trading decisions. However, traders who want to include sentiment into their trading process should keep in mind that these signals are ultra-short-term in nature, meaning they are best applied in intraday trading strategies. Additionally, it is highly important to define a clear stop strategy to protect against unnecessary losses.

More and more institutions have started to include sentiment data in their decision processes. This is not limited to institutions and organisations which are primarily actors in the financial market, like hedge funds, asset managers, or banks. Retail companies strongly rely on product ratings (e.g. Amazon stars) for their ordering decisions. Travel agencies monitor hotel ratings at Trip Advisor (www.tripadvisor.com) to optimise their marketing, e.g. through promoting highly rated hotels in their search engines. These are only two examples showing the strongly increasing importance of sentiment data for nearly all business areas.

As founders of a company specialised in sentiment retrieval, we go one step further and predict that in less than five years from August 2013 it will be mandatory to monitor market sentiment for all participants in the financial markets, at least if they want to make sound trading and investment decisions.

Like technical analysis, which was a tool for professional investors at first, sentiment data will become one of the key fundamentals for asset valuation on a short- to mid-term basis (Figure 6). Those leaving out this important metric will make worse trading and investment decisions as they ignore a major influence factor for short-term price building.

Figure 6 – asset valuation in the future

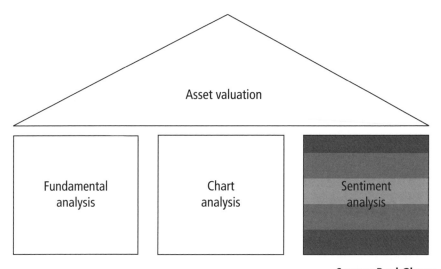

Source: Raul Glavan

Behind closed doors professional asset managers and hedge funds already leverage the predictive power of sentiment data for their trading models. Companies like StockPulse (www.stockpulse.de) are the spearhead for making this data available to a broader audience.

REFERENCES

Krauss, J., Nann, S. and Schoder, D., 'Towards Universal Sentiment Analysis through Web Mining', Poster Session, European Conference on Information Systems, Barcelona, Spain (2012)

Nann, S., Krauss, J. and Schoder, D., 'Predictive Analytics on Public Data – the Case of Stock Markets', European Conference on Information Systems, Utrecht, Netherlands (2013)

Yerva, Surender Reddy, Miklós, Zoltán and Aberer, Karl 'It was easy, when apples and blackberries were only fruits', EPFL working paper, retrieved 30/03/2013 infoscience.epfl.ch/record/151616/files/LSIR_WePS3_Paper.pdf (2010).

ENDNOTES

[1] Daily Sentiment Trader is a daily newsletter with signals calculated on sentiment data from social media published by StockPulse each trading day.

[2] Pulse Picks is the software engine used by StockPulse for calculating trading signals from sentiment data.

THE STORY OF OANDA: BUILDING A COMPANY IN THE FINANCE INDUSTRY

BY RICHARD OLSEN

ABOUT THE AUTHOR

Richard Olsen has combined academic research with hands-on experience in financial markets. He founded Olsen & Associates in 1985, which has developed and marketed a real-time information system with forecasts and trading recommendations for financial markets. He is co-founder of OANDA, a successful internet market maker, and Olsen Ltd, a hedge fund. He has recently founded Lykke Corp, a crowd-based asset management company.

Richard is a pioneer of high frequency finance and co-authored the book *Introduction to High Frequency Finance*, published by Academic Press in 2001. Together with a team of researchers he has recently discovered 12 new scaling laws of the foreign exchange markets, continuing work on scaling laws that was first started in 1989. He is visiting professor at the Centre for Computational Finance and Economic Agents at the University of Essex.

INTRODUCTION

INTERNET TECHNOLOGY HAS paved the way for a number of great new companies, like Amazon, Facebook and Google. Why have we not seen major internet game-changers in finance? Are there obstacles that make it particularly difficult, if not impossible, in this field?

What follows is my attempt at finding answers to these essential questions. As co-founder of OANDA, established in 1996, I report my experience of creating an internet finance company – more specifically, an internet foreign exchange market maker.

THE UNIQUE SELLING PROPOSITION OF THE INTERNET

In the mid-nineties many of us thought that the financial industry was the ideal candidate for internet technology. What stood at the basis of this assumption was the fact that finance is not a brick and mortar industry. In reality, markets are virtual and they are all about information transmission. If one trades currencies on a bank account and sells $1m for euro, then this $1m is a mere bookkeeping entry in the trading system of the bank and does not have a physical existence as, for example, a house one buys for the same amount.

In terms of the total transacted dollar amount, the financial industry is the biggest of all. The Bank of International Settlement (BIS) estimated that in October 2012 the average daily foreign exchange turnover was around $5 trillion. This represents one-third of the annual US Gross Domestic Product. Intra-day transaction volumes are gigantic. However, these transactions do not deal with real objects that can be seen or touched; they only represent information messages that are exchanged between computers.

In our present world, the workflow of the business processes that dictate how financial transactions are conducted still follows rules that were established in an era when transactions represented concrete actions. In those times all financial exchanges were recorded in writing, with written confirmations produced and delivered days after the transaction was over. Even though traders transact at a pace of milliseconds, settlement still occurs two business days later, or even longer for certain markets.

This represents a contradiction of facts. The outdated business process leads to the increase of operational costs and causes inefficiencies in the financial markets, characterised by systematic mispricing and higher price volatility. According to National Income and Product Accounts, the financial industry in the US accounts for only 8% of GDP, but generates a third of all profits. It is the operational inefficiency mentioned above that has allowed the financial industry to boost their profitability.

In spite of its unique selling proposition, why have we not yet seen in the financial world any big success stories that have blown competitors away by leveraging the internet? I will continue my attempt at providing an answer to this question by explaining what my colleagues and I learned when we built OANDA.

HOW I STARTED MY CAREER IN FINANCE

Way back in the early 1980s I worked for a Swiss private bank, initially in the research department and as a foreign exchange trader afterward. That was in the early days of computers, when banks had just started to get access to databases of daily historical data of equities, bonds and other financial instruments. My task was to extract information from a database at the request of researchers, portfolio managers and customers. They used this information to make more informed investment decisions. It is common knowledge that success in banking and investment management depends on the quality of the information available. With access to better information systems it is possible to achieve a more consistent performance.

It was while working as a researcher that I spotted a business opportunity. *Time* magazine had reported the first success stories in Silicon Valley and I wanted to emulate their success in Switzerland. As a result, in 1985 I founded Olsen & Associates. My objective was to leverage computer technology to build a real-time information system, with forecasts and trading recommendations for decision makers in banks and other financial institutions. My dream was that the system would have tick-by-tick price information and forecasts ranging from minutes to hours, weeks and months, including real-time trading recommendations and other analytical tools. In addition, everything was to be graphics-based. However, I failed to take into consideration that the environment was not conducive to tech startups at the time.

Today, with smartphones and slick user interfaces, it is hardly conceivable why such a goal should have been a big provocation. However, in those times we were faced with huge challenges. First and foremost, the connection with our customers was made through fixed communication land lines that we had to rent for tens of thousands of dollars per year. In contrast, nowadays an internet connection costs next to nothing.

Secondly, in 1985 the hardware cost to store one gigabyte of information was around $100,000, compared to the cost of one cent today. To make things worse, we started out thinking that it was going to be a three-month endeavour and only gradually did we realise that we were working on a project of a completely different scale. However, after several false starts we scored a reasonable success and, by the mid-90s, we were able to win over 70 mid-sized to large banks all over Europe.

We positioned Olsen & Associates as a thought leader with hands-on experience in analysing tick-by-tick price information in currency markets. Slowly, we managed to build a strong and unique brand, well-known and widely used in the high frequency trading world. As a result, in 1995 we hosted the first high frequency finance conference and provided academics with free access to a large set of tick-by-tick historical market data. In those days that was unheard of. The event was attended by participants from around the world and it scored a big success. At the same time, this conference helped establish a new field of research, what today is called *market microstructure*.

By then we knew we had been successful in establishing a strong brand. However, the truth that we had to face was that we had been unable to attain critical mass, and, as a result, we had not been able to commercialise our exciting technology to its full potential.

OANDA: INFORMATION COMPANY AND MARKET MAKER

It was at the 1995 high frequency finance conference that my school friend, Michael Stumm, suggested that we build a currency converter and make our currency data available for free. Michael, who was also on the board of Olsen & Associates, was an early evangelist of the internet.

At Olsen & Associates leading banks were buying our tick data for six digit figures. In contrast, here we were, deciding to offer a free service over the internet that would cannibalise at least part of our market. In spite of this apparent contradiction, Michael and I founded a new company, named OANDA (an abbreviation of Olsen & Associates), as an internet offshoot to do exactly that.

The OANDA currency converter was an instant success and attracted customers from around the world. Among our early subscribers was AOL, who paid top money to white label our currency converter. The run-of-the-mill customer would link our currency converter to their website as a free service and we would be able to sell the advertising space. Nevertheless, we did not want OANDA to be a mere information company.

From my experience with Olsen & Associates I had learned about the pitfalls of being an information company. I did not foresee that this business model would be problematic. Banks price dump information services as a teaser to get customers to trade on their own. It is this very aspect that makes the trading business highly lucrative, as banks can embed their fees in transaction prices so that transaction costs are not readily visible to customers. The average banking customer does not appreciate the importance of low transaction costs and does not realise that these costs add up and multiply with every transaction. Thus, banks were not really motivated to use our services and it turned out that Olsen & Associates was locked into the information business. With OANDA I was convinced I wanted to move away from being an information-based business and turn into a finance player.

At the time, banks were charging their customers wide spreads of 0.3% to 0.5% for currency trading. In contrast, institutional traders at top banks were paying 0.03%. Our plan was to build a market maker with razor thin spreads, a real mass product with a low price point, which previously had only been available to the best institutional customers. The key hypothesis in our reasoning process was very simple: if we managed to attract enough customers, the buy and sell flow would then net out and we would earn our living by keeping the spread.

With OANDA we were going to build a very transparent platform. Every trade, whatever the size of the ticket, be it one or a million dollars, would be executed at the same price. Generally banks charge different spreads for different ticket sizes, which creates a lot of confusion for the trader. By offering the same spread to all our customers we were sending out the message that they were trading with a company that offered the same fair deal to everyone.

We launched our trading platform in 2001 with a spread of 0.04%. Over time we actually ended up reducing the spread to 0.006% for EURUSD. Our product proved to be an instant success. Customers started to sign up even before the platform was officially released. What made all this possible was the strong brand name that we had built with our currency converter, which had actually become the industry standard that literally everyone used. I can say that it was this tool that made us respectable and gave us credibility. This was something that had not happened before. Until then, the fact that a simple tool like a currency converter could actually project an image of solidity and give traders the confidence to deposit money with OANDA had been unheard of.

SECOND-BY-SECOND INTEREST PAYMENTS

Apart from the low spread and the absence of price discrimination, the OANDA trading platform introduced another novelty in the industry: we pay and charge interest by the second, not just on a daily basis as is the practice in the industry. At OANDA interest is only charged for the period of time that the traded positions remain open, regardless of the length of time involved, be it a few minutes, a few hours or a few days.

This is not the case in today's financial industry, where interest is charged for a minimum increment of one business day and with no interest charged for shorter time increments. If a position is opened and closed before the end of the same trading day, no interest is paid or charged. In contrast, if a position is opened just for a few minutes before the end of the trading day and closed immediately after the start of the following trading day, the interest is charged for a full 24-hour day. This way of doing business seemed natural when trades were processed manually and trade confirmations were hand delivered. In reality, banks have hardwired their procedures in their mainframe computers so that they can rely on batch processing. This does not leave them much flexibility on how interest is charged, even though this may be detrimental to some investors and beneficial to others.

The difference between daily and second-by-second interest payment is not an operational nicety. The archaic way of doing business distorts price actions in certain markets and it can even impact whole economies. For example, currencies bearing high interest rates move on a higher trajectory interrupted by painful selloffs. In liquid markets where 80% of the transaction volume are trades which are opened and closed in less than 20 minutes, small price differences have a big impact.

WHAT WERE THE CHALLENGES AT OANDA?

RETAIL TRADERS LOSE MONEY

We had wanted to turn OANDA into a really big market maker but, even though the company was highly successful, we did not reach our objective. The truth of the matter is that we remained a retail broker and did not successfully penetrate the institutional market. It was true that OANDA offered its customers much lower spreads than a regular broker. This was good news for our customers, who lost money more slowly than traders with other brokers. However, OANDA customers were losing money nevertheless. I did not like the fact that we were marketing a product where the average customer was losing money on a regular basis. We had wanted to build a tool that would make trading safer and more profitable, but, unfortunately, we did not deliver on that promise.

The OANDA trading platform had been conceived as a large-scale research laboratory where we could study trading behaviour in real time and figure out the deeper laws of finance. In reality, we did not get around to even starting to address this problem in earnest. We got stuck midway in creating the next generation product, which would have transformed the OANDA platform into a win-win proposition for its customers. This was a real shame.

OPERATIONAL SAFETY

When we built OANDA we were confronted with all the obvious challenges of building a business: raising the necessary capital, getting the right team of people, launching the product and creating the right marketing spin. These are common problems that any entrepreneur faces. The question arises, then, whether our challenges may have been different because we were operating in the financial industry.

Starting a business in finance is far more difficult than in any other industry because the commodity is real money. If anything goes wrong, the penalties can be immense. There are plenty of examples of companies that got heavily burned. Take that of Knight Capital, who, in 2012, lost $440m within 40 minutes because a software engineer released a new trading software but an old testing program got activated instead. The result is that this testing program went wild buying and selling at erroneous prices and their losses were enormous.

The risk of meltdowns implies that garage operations do not really work in finance. In addition, operational risk can stifle creativity, which explains why finance companies turn conservative. It is actually difficult to be otherwise, because technical innovation has to be coupled with strong operational capabilities.

GETTING THE RIGHT TALENT

Another major obstacle to launching a finance company is getting the right talent. By definition, internet finance companies have to do business differently from traditional banks and other financial institutions. They have to build products that are fully automated and cannot rely on human beings to do the actual trading. In contrast, a traditional bank hires a trader to do the trading. The problem is that, in most cases, that trader will not be able to provide a rational explanation as to why they trade the way they do. In order to get a computer to do the work of a trader, it is necessary to create algorithms to mimic their actions. The problem is that these algorithms can only be written by somebody who thoroughly understands the business.

Unfortunately, it is very hard to find these people. Universities do not seem to provide the appropriate expertise as there are hardly any professors with hands-on experience in the nuts and bolts of finance. As a result, university graduates do not have the right training and, therefore, there is a lack of real talent for building a true technology company in finance.

REGULATORY OBSTACLES

The finance industry is heavily regulated. These regulations should safeguard the markets and the general public from any misbehaviour. In actual fact, they do a lot to cement the existing structure of financial markets, which gives big institutions a decisive competitive edge. Newcomers cannot launch new business models because regulations impose large capital requirements and other restrictions. The experimental approach to new business models of internet companies in many other sectors cannot be copied in finance. It takes a real insider, who knows all the gory details of regulations and other institutional obstacles, to come up with a truly innovative and successful business model that ticks off all the right regulatory boxes. It is unlikely that a university graduate will launch the right business out of sheer luck.

THE FUTURE

I believe that the challenges that we encountered at OANDA are not unique, but, in fact, quite common in the financial industry as a whole. The industry follows antiquated procedures and is immobilised by unwieldy regulations and an outdated structure. Whoever can break this deadlock will reap a windfall.

The institutional insiders are the only ones who know all the operational details and, at the same time, have a deep understanding of market mechanics. My guess is that eventually an insider will come up with a revolutionary business model that will turn the industry upside down. I think that the coming years will be full of change.

Finance provides unique opportunities for angel investors. If they pick the real game-changer they can make huge profits, but, even more interestingly, they can help make financial markets more efficient and the economic system more sustainable, which is not a bad thing.

RECOVERING LOST TRUST

BY PAUL D. STALLARD

ABOUT THE AUTHOR

Paul D. Stallard is CEO of Hurndall-Stallard Associates Limited, a business strategy, business development and marketing communications consultancy specialising in retail financial services. Paul works with top UK and international brands in Savings and Loans, Asset Management, Wealth Management, Retail Banking, Private Banking, Derivative Trading and Stock Broking.

DAMAGED BEYOND REPAIR?

THIS PAPER STUDIES how key decisions made by financial services companies up to 30 years ago have resulted in the situation today where they are not trusted, they are not believed and where their customers feel totally disenfranchised. The paper also includes a series of mini case studies and suggests what might be done to repair the situation going forward. The case studies are based on real-life experiences. They are not meant to disparage or embarrass, but more to show that we are all able to learn from such experiences. Hopefully, the outcome will be customers who feel more confident in the companies providing the financial products and services they use.

The financial services industry has damaged its image and reputation among the consuming public beyond a level ever imagined possible some three decades ago. It is not always healthy to dwell on the past, just as it is unhealthy to listen to people wearing rose tinted spectacles talk about how good banking was in the old days. The answer to making the retail financial services space better today and in the future is not about making it as it was in the past; that is neither possible nor desirable.

It may be a cliché but the golden rule to getting customers to trust you is to treat them with respect and not to take them for fools, because they are not. Do not do to them what you would not have done to yourself. Instead, listen to them regularly and continually treat them how the best companies treat their customers. There is nothing wrong with copying the excellence of other organisations, but remember in doing so that this applies to the whole business and not just front-line staff.

UNINTENDED CONSEQUENCES

On the 27 October 1986 the financial services landscape in the UK changed forever. Labelled Big Bang, it was the day Margaret Thatcher's government deregulated financial markets. The effect of this soon became apparent to the British when companies they had been dealing with for years (banks, building societies, insurance companies) suddenly started selling them each others' products and services and doing it badly.

> Shortly after Big Bang the director of a large financial services organisation told his head of marketing he wanted a letter sent to 500,000 customers selling them a personal loan. The head of marketing pointed out that sending out a standard letter to 500,000 customers would be a rather crude, costly and highly ineffective way of selling something to customers who do not expect to get a personal loan from their building society.
>
> Despite this sound and proven advice no attempt at segmentation or profiling was allowed; there was no testing, indeed nothing special in the offer and no follow-up of any kind. Not surprisingly, three weeks after the mailing landed on doormats around the country the head of marketing was summoned by the director and carpeted for not being very good at marketing, given that only two loans had been requested. Furthermore he was told he was not to engage in any further direct mail activity on behalf of the business.
>
> The director was clearly in the wrong for not heeding the advice of his marketing expert; the very least he could have done is ask for evidence that what the head of marketing was saying was true.

The Thatcher government gave birth to Big Bang because the once dominant City of London financial institutions were struggling to compete with foreign banks and it was thought a huge and favourable change could be effected in the shape and structure of the market with an increase in overall market activity. Yet the government overlooked or misread the situation; if the British bankers were having trouble competing with foreign banks pre Big Bang how were they going to perform in a hugely more competitive market afterwards?

> In the run-up to deregulation an American came to the UK to explain the effects of financial services deregulation from the US point of view, given they experienced much the same change some ten years previously. Basically, he said we should prepare ourselves for years of change and uncertainty but his words which resonated most in the mind were "You will not know what deregulation has done to your industry for years and years to come." We all now know how right he was!

Considering the short-sighted government intentions with Big Bang it may not be surprising that in 2010 when questioned by BBC Radio 4, Nigel Lawson, Margaret Thatcher's Chancellor in 1986, said the current global financial crisis that began in 2007 and which is still with us today was an unintended consequence of Big Bang.

WHAT THE CONSUMER SAW

The Thatcher government thought the two biggest problems behind the decline in British banking were over-regulation and the power behind the *old boy network* among bankers; it was convinced that a totally free market where competition and meritocracy were dominant would solve the problem.

Sadly, from a shareholder's or consumer's point of view, free market competition did not always deliver what was hoped for.

> Sometime after Big Bang when the implications of what had happened sunk in, a large national building society thought it a good idea to go into estate agency. So, it spent in excess of £30m buying a chain of estate agents. It appointed an internal candidate to run the newly formed subsidiary company who when asked about his vision for the company going forward, how they were going to make their mark, etc., said "We will imbue the estate agency with a building society type service." Only a few years later, with no profit to speak of, the estate agency chain was sold back to its original owners for a fraction of what it had been bought for.

> A quick analysis of each market should have been carried out to show that it would never be possible to make money by injecting a warm, mutual and almost philanthropic building society business model into that of an estate agency business. Estate agency is a highly competitive and cut-throat business, where tension is high between those selling, those buying property and all those in between the two helping them conclude contractual arrangements.

Forget the customer at your peril when exercising mega-changes in the direction or the type of services provided because success takes an extraordinarily long time to plan and bring about. Generally speaking it takes as long to get consumers into a position to respond positively to a new product as it takes to plan the launch of the product. Equally, a company may be able to acquire or build a new service in a relatively short period of time but that matters little to consumers who only know them for providing something else.

REGULATION

It is possible to be simplistic about regulation and pose the notion that if financial services companies looked after their customers properly, if they only sold them what was needed and what was right for them, if they willingly provided redress when it was proven their advice was incorrect at the time it was given, etc., then regulation would not be needed.

However, in a highly competitive, ever-changing and increasingly complex financial world there is need for regulation. Although most companies openly and honestly tackle these challenges, the complex nature of the markets attracts undesirable if not blatantly illegal behaviour where the ultimate victim will always be the consumer. Therefore such a market demands strong regulation to bring a sense of order, control, fairness and propriety. It is crucial that the regulated and the regulator respect each other's role in delivering a healthy financial services market and ultimate satisfaction to an ever demanding public.

Shortly after deregulation in 1986 one of the handful of regulators that were set up to oversee different sub-sectors of the financial services market held a conference in London. In his opening address to delegates the head of this organisation said, "We need regulation to stop you lot ripping off your clients." One justifiably disgruntled delegate vehemently objected to the comment, saying he thought the gentleman was grossly insulting and totally out of order for suggesting that he rips-off his clients and he asked that the remark be withdrawn.

This was not the right way for a regulator to set out building a strong working relationship with the industry, especially as this was a hugely sensitive time for everyone concerned. There is no doubt that the speaker should have been more professional, less arrogant and he should not have assumed that because a handful of IFAs had been found guilty of some misdemeanour against their clients all other IFAs were likely to be guilty of doing the same thing.

Regulators have to continually up their game to ensure they fully understand and are prepared to tackle the smallest detail and the complex nature of both the markets and the products they are regulating. They also need to do this because globally the financial services industry attracts some of the very best minds (actuaries, strategists, product engineers, etc.) that education systems can deliver. Sometimes the sector attracts people with great ability but an even greater need to make money dishonestly by employing devious or misleading tactics and profiting at someone else's expense. As we increasingly see, more and more of these criminal miscreants are being caught and subjected to even greater levels of punishment.

At a corporate level making a lot of money from products which have not been tested properly or seen to stand the test of time is a sign of professional incompetence, but intentionally setting out to deceive is criminal. Through their regulatory authorities, governments and the voting public will demand that professional incompetence, criminality and dishonesty in the sector are not only dealt with most severely but also that it is largely eradicated so as to bring confidence back to the personal finance sector.

COMPETITION

Prior to deregulation in 1986 and compared with today, competition in the financial services market was such a dignified, genteel process and in many ways it did not exist. Bank managers were known to actively recommend customers move money from their current accounts to building societies because the latter paid higher rates of interest on deposits than banks.

On 27 October 1986 all that changed. More or less overnight serious unrelenting competition arrived as financial services companies were able to sell each other's products and services. One of the most significant effects of increased competition was that shareholders, boards of directors and senior management quickly realised the potential for greater profits, to the extent that their expectations created a pressure to sell like never before. Every business in this sector changed from managing the ups and downs in expected market share to an all out attack to sell more products to existing customers. The only problem with this was few financial services companies knew how to go about it properly for they had no previous experience and they did not employ sales people.

However, those weaknesses did not stop them adopting a strong selling orientation throughout their businesses. In many companies poor sales performance created even stronger pressures to use not just attractive sales incentives but fear tactics too, that is "meet your targets or lose your job."

Good salesmanship is not something that can be learnt overnight. The sales profession favours people with a positive, pleasant, out-going and can-do demeanour, but even they need training. Whilst it is easy to sell products and services to people who clearly want and need them, it is something completely different to employ crude, untrained attempts at selling products to customers who patently do not need or want them. Adopting such tactics quickly reduces the legitimacy of customer relationships and arguably to this very day we see many companies facing the full force of their customer's anger and complete puzzlement as to why they have been and continue to be treated in this way.

> In the late 1980s a building society launched an incentive-based campaign in its branches to sell a ten-year tax efficient regular savings account. The campaign went well until the son of a 96-year-old lady complained that his mother was not allowed to leave the branch until she opened a ten-year regular savings account! This was clearly a spectacular example of mis-selling. Regardless of whether the customer would still have been alive in ten years' time, she had no need for regular savings or tax efficient money management. She was a soft target to increase sales performance by staff who should have known better.

Selling is a highly respected and skilled profession that requires constant practice and improvement in execution. It does not suit everyone but whatever job a person performs it must by definition touch a customer somewhere, somehow, sometime, therefore such customer contact must be part of the selling process. The future highly successful company will be the one which successfully engages all staff in a constant process of customer understanding – appreciating why customers buy from the company, when, how and for what purpose.

PRODUCT PROLIFERATION

If there is one fundamental sin that financial services companies have been guilty of since deregulation it is that instead of making products and services they knew customers wanted and needed, they have created the products *they* wanted to make and sell. Many companies are guilty of making products and services they wanted to sell because it is easier, cheaper or the opportunity for profit is greater. They have then attempted to force customers to buy them with strong-arm tactics, short-term discounts, gimmicks or shear weight of advertising spend.

Many companies thought their long-term relationship with customers was determined by the quantity of the products and services they sold to them. They thought the strength of their brand would allow them to sell more products to more customers, which in turn would ensure a greater degree of customer loyalty. In banking the process of providing all the products and services a customer could need is called Bank Assurance and it has not worked. If only the banks had really taken the time to find out how customers actually behave they would have discovered that in an increasingly competitive market, knowledgeable, savvy and confident customers tend to compartmentalise their buying behaviour, getting the best from different companies and not being concerned about brand loyalty.

Seriously underestimating the intelligence of customers is a grave error. Customers know when they are being sold to. What are they to think when their bank goes into overdrive selling at every conceivable opportunity yet they can easily recall instances within the recent past when their bank did not support them or help them overcome a difficult time? Whilst customers know when the economy is in good shape and understand the commercial facts of life, they do not hold these economic circumstances in mind when they make transactions as consumers – instead they will remember the hurt of being treated in what they perceive to be a bad, uncalled for manner. Customers want help from a bank when they need help, not when the bank wants to offer help, decides it can afford to give it or sets out to sell it to them.

> Many commentators have said previously that people who lead financial services companies, especially banks, should only do so if they have spent a reasonable period of time actually working with customers. This is not at all unreasonable and it will become a requirement going forward because the chances of securing a robust and successful financial services sector in the UK must be greatly enhanced if, all other things being equal (experience, academic achievements, etc.), the CEO actually knows how real people think and behave when dealing with their personal finances.

MARKETING COMMUNICATIONS

Ever since financial companies first started using formal marketing practices in the late 1970s, marketing professionals have failed to show their executive bosses and peers just how the marketing communication process really works. They may not have totally understood it themselves at the time, but regardless of this what we saw was the development of an expectation that business would flow as soon as advertising commenced and the degree of new business produced would be in proportion to how much was spent on advertising. Such expectations are largely still with us today but in recent years two further events have significantly affected the communications process between companies and their stakeholders, especially customers.

The first is the almost inexorable fragmentation of the media where more and more channels of communication have opened up, particularly as a result of the internet and the development of high-quality broadcast media. Media fragmentation has meant companies have been able to deliver specific marketing messages to highly targeted groups of customers using very precise language and images, knowing they will resonate with the particular group of people they are talking to.

However, the second event – with arguably the greatest effect on the communications process – has been the arrival of the digital age. Social media has given companies the ability to maintain an on-going dialogue, a conversation no less, with customers or target customers that has previously not been possible.

THE MARKETING COMMUNICATION GAP

Set against a background where there is still an expectation of immediate results from marketing activity, there is in many companies a gap between those holding responsibility for signing-off marketing expenditure and those whose job it is to plan and recommend how budgets are used. The former group are often older executive types and whilst they are more experienced in business, they do not appreciate how new age media works. The latter group, however, are likely to be younger and absolutely steeped in where the media revolution is happening. Very often the first group have difficulty understanding what the second group is talking about.

On the face of it the communication gap should be bridged over time as people age and move on, but of course it never will be. It is reasonable to assume that there will often be a significant gap in the knowledge, experience and familiarity with new ways of doing things between the old and the new or younger people in any business. Ambitious, driven companies must attend to such gaps because they will not close naturally.

Currently consumers are increasing their use of digital media at a prodigious rate; failure to acknowledge this by acting upon it now will not be forgiven by shareholders in the future. Businesses today where the board and executive management close their eyes and ears to the ways of the world (social media, etc.) will quickly go into decline and leave the door wide open for the more technologically and digitally attuned business to step through.

MORE EFFECTIVE COMMUNICATIONS

The effect of so many financial services companies being very product oriented results in the directional nature and tone of their customer communication being phrased on a company-out basis, full of phrases such as "We have done this" or "You will be delighted to hear" or "I am happy to announce". An organisation which is truly customer oriented will phrase the direction of its communications on the basis of customer-in, for example "Knowing that you value" or "Your need for".

Effective communication is a two-way, information sharing process which involves one party sending a message that is easily understood by the receiving party. Tomorrow's highly successful financial services business will be the one where everyone working in the business, at every level, constantly checks and validates the meaning and direction of what they write and say. Fast, efficient, digitally-led media fragmentation will demand that clear and accurate communication becomes a fundamental corporate ethos – as central as the principle of treating customers fairly – and it too should be led by the person at the very top of the organisation.

Not understanding how the marketing communications process works and constantly being told that digital media permits more immediate, meaningful and highly-targeted communications with the target audience leaves the executives with a problem. Many fail to appreciate that buying a financial services product is not an impulse purchase; it is not like buying a chocolate bar at the supermarket checkout.

Buying an investment product, whether via an advisor or not, takes time and consideration. People have to get used to the idea, they may swot up on the product, compare it with others in the market or sit and watch its performance over time before they decide to invest. People will not invest because someone writes to them and tells them it is a good idea to do so. Similarly, wise people will not invest in companies they have never heard of.

So, all these issues buzzing around in the head of a potential buyer need addressing and they take time to resolve. The very essence of the buying process centres on an individual going through at least four stages of communication:

1. Getting their attention.
2. Generating interest in what is being sold.
3. Creating the desire to buy.
4. Getting them to take action.

It is rare indeed to achieve all four stages in one communication. In most cases it takes numerous communications to close the sale. Generally speaking the more complicated the product or service, the more customer contacts are needed.

Boards of directors and their executives must be persuaded to understand that diligently, patiently and respectfully communicating with consumers on subjects they are interested in will build confidence and trust in the business. Perhaps time, competitive pressure and continual professional development will close the gap once the two ends of the marketing management spectrum work more closely together. When that happens the business should expect spectacularly impressive results.

Probably the most clever and much respected organisation in this sector is the one who knows exactly how many communications they must effect before someone making an enquiry actually buys the product they enquired about. Someone making an enquiry is put into a pool of contacts that are subject to a pre-planned series of communications at set intervals which take the enquirer along a path of Attention, Awareness, Desire and Action. That it has taken them days, weeks months or years to get the business is irrelevant now; their initial investment has paid off and it continues to pay-off at a cost much less than the ensuing revenue. In marketing terms this is called *product management* – very good product management.

CUSTOMER KNOWLEDGE AND CONSUMERISM

It is no surprise today that we see so much focus on protecting the rights of customers given the extremely high level of competition in the market. However, it is surprising that the people doing all the protecting of consumers and their rights are not the people in companies who are asking consumers to entrust them with their wealth.

The most commonly asked investor question today is "How safe is my money?" In light of the current global economic crisis and the continual avalanche of new products and services this is understandable.

From the point of view of UK investors the medium to long-term effects of the current global financial crisis are unclear, just as they are to the British government. However, as a result of the crisis the government is struggling to balance the nation's books as it endeavours to keep the economy going and encourage growth. For these reasons the government is reducing the overall level of financial support to the population as a whole in order to save money to pay-off the huge national debt left over by the crisis.

At the same time, all UK companies are under severe pressure to remain competitive, especially against the low level cost of production in the developing world. To combat these pressures many companies have already and continue to reduce their costs by closing down company pension schemes, holding back pay rises, revising contracts of employment and generally reducing other benefits they were providing previously. This means employees now have to carefully consider what financial arrangements should be made to provide for their long-term future and during the many years of retirement – where, how and what is the best way to save for the long term?

All in all, the British investor today must feel a really lonely person. He is worried about whether his money is safe wherever it is invested and he is worried about who he can trust because every time he hears or reads the news there is a story about someone going to jail for embezzling client money or mis-selling investment or insurance products. No one seems to have a proven, coherent argument as to where exactly he should save for the long term, for when he retires.

So, we should not be surprised he feels on his own. Little wonder more and more consumers are learning about how to manage their own investments and little wonder they become extremely litigious when something goes wrong.

> Some years ago the chief executive of a financial services company was persuaded to sit in on a number of customer focus groups to learn what customers were saying about his company's products. He was introduced to each group as a member of the research company and it was said he was not there to participate but to make notes. For many, many days after the focus groups the only thing the CEO could talk about was what his customers would say about this, that and the other. Overnight he became a disciple of his customers; his focus and enthusiasm for doing what was right for his customers was contagious for a while.

> The difficulty was persuading him to keep going to such groups or making any other kind of real customer contact going forward. He thought his one-off personal epiphany was all that was needed for him to make sure his customers were looked after forevermore. He completely missed the point of the need to constantly keep in touch with customers. Over time his view of customer needs and wants became increasingly out of date.

Companies in the UK must realise they cannot expect to regain the support and trust of customers without drastic action. Pandering, shallow promises or any action which is seen as an attempt to pull the wool over the eyes will not work. Many organisations have allowed the situation to become so bad, so unprofitable, that they need to make some significant and costly gesture to bring customers back on-side.

Costly does not necessarily mean financially costly; it could for example mean bringing democratically elected customers into the boardroom or setting up customer panels. It could mean making the whole business and its affairs completely transparent to the investigation of anyone who has a vested interest in the management of the resources it consumes.

A meaningful customer-oriented approach to marketing and maintaining simple, safe and secure financial products will go a long way to restoring the faith customers have in financial services companies. Such companies must open up a direct communication channel with their customers and the first people to listen and talk with customers must be the people who make the decisions – the CEO, COO, etc. The customer must be made to feel he is King once more.

MANAGEMENT EXPERIENCE

The most inexcusable action of executive management in the financial services sector during the past 20 years or so was the decision to retire early so many of their most senior and most experienced managers.

The rationale for doing this made perfect sense economically for they were the most expensive group of employees and would take a healthy cost element out of the business. However, some 20 years on we have much evidence to show that such cost savings were short-lived. For example, the day a 50-year-old bank manager walked out of his office for the last time, on a full pension and healthcare package, was the day banks began to damage their reputation and success at lending to small and medium-sized businesses; it was the day they began to lose the trust of their customers.

The recently retired and very experienced bank manager was replaced by a young and much cheaper banker with a degree, lots of enthusiasm and self belief, but absolutely no experience of what it was like dealing with small businesses. Someone in head office whose idea this was and who also probably had no experience of dealing with real customers had deduced that all the new manager had to do was follow the bank's lending guidelines to the letter and the bank's risk would be minimised. One wonders how many businesses over the years did not get off the ground or survive for lack of much needed capital and an experienced bank manager who knew the people involved and who understood the business.

As he neared his 50th birthday a bank manager was asked by his boss if he wished to take early retirement. The bank offered a full pension, which meant an index-linked annual pension equivalent to two-thirds of his final salary (which was in excess of £100,000 p.a.). With private healthcare included in the package it was not a difficult decision and the bank manager duly took his retirement on his 50th birthday and decided to live in sunnier climes.

Some two years later the extremely happy, less stressed and far healthier ex-bank manager received a telephone call from his ex-boss in London. He was calling to ask if he would come back to work because the bank had realised the error of its ways in letting so many experienced senior managers retire early. His boss said money would not be a problem – he would be paid more than when he left and he could work anywhere in the UK, it was his choice. In other words the bank would really make it worth his while. The one-time bank manager said "I have just been fishing, I have enough money thanks, I am perfectly happy, healthy and relaxed so please tell me why I would want to come back to work at the bank."

Tomorrow's excellent companies will of course remain free to manage their employment policies and strategies in terms of cost, age and experience, but they will do so having regard for the medium to long-term implications of their actions. Experience will become a highly prized and much sought after criterion when recruiting staff. These requirements will be coupled with a drive to constantly update skills and knowledge and a sea-change in attitude will render the older and comparatively more expensive employee absolutely essential.

Similarly, companies and their supporting organisations (trade bodies, training institutions) will devise more ways to invest in and build on employee skills and experiences. Continual professional development will evolve to the point that anyone working in financial services will have to be licensed and that licence will have to be renewed on a regular basis via some form of mandatory check or examination.

EPILOGUE

Much is made today about the quality of CEOs working in British financial companies, particularly the banks. Notwithstanding the march of time and ever-changing market conditions and economic circumstances, it is a fact that many of the CEOs who successfully guided their institutions into being some of the largest, strongest and most successful in the world were people who had been with their company for a very long time.

They would have joined the bank at a very early age, risen through the ranks and if they were lucky they would have been spotted and subjected to a special career development programme as suitable candidates for high office in the bank. Those that made it all the way to the top would have stayed for as long as they were able before retiring on a very good and well deserved pension.

Today's CEO tends to be a high flyer from outside the bank or a relative newcomer in the bank. He negotiates a very high six or seven-figure salary, lots of benefits, a big bonus, share options, a pension, healthcare, etc., and a contract for, say, up to five years. He has no ingrained loyalty to the bank and is probably looking forward to retiring on the proceeds of his CEO's position at the end of his contract, if not before.

The difference between the two is the former is encouraged to think more strategically about what the bank should do for its customers on a long-term basis. He understands and has seen most market cycles come and go and he knows that today's problem area is tomorrow's source of exceedingly good profit.

Conversely, the more short-term occupant of the CEO's chair is more likely to favour strategies and tactics which make quick profits and/or reduce costs by significant degrees so as to hit his own bonus plan target, to please stakeholders and in particular to delight shareholders by issuing above average dividend yield.

There is something seriously wrong if financial institutions are not currently executing extensive succession planning programmes throughout their businesses to ensure homegrown CEOs and other executives take over the top jobs.

2

THE DIGITAL REVOLUTION AND ITS EFFECT ON FINANCIAL SERVICES DISTRIBUTION AND COMMUNICATION

THE FOURFOLD REVOLUTION IN FINANCIAL SERVICES

BY SCOTT BALES

ABOUT THE AUTHOR

Scott Bales is the global leader on innovation, trends, design and mobility. He is a thought leader who thrives on the intersection between cultural and behavioural changes with technology innovations. He is Chief Mobile Officer for Moven, the world's first ever card-less bank. Scott is a self-proclaimed extrovert who has meshed a fascination with people and what motivates them with his enthusiasm for technology. He currently runs the Asia Pacific office of boutique advisory firm, User Strategy, in Singapore. With over ten years of international experience in innovation, thought leadership, implementation planning, and strategy, he is a soughtafter consultant and speaker who communicates his unorthodox ideas with passion and charisma. Scott has a Bachelor of Applied Science, a postgraduate Diploma in Information Technology and a Masters of Business from Swinburne University of Technology.

COMING TO TERMS WITH THE REVOLUTION

IN THE PAST decade digital has slowly but surely worked its way into every aspect of our daily lives, including commerce, lifestyle, communication, how we interact with brands and – importantly – how we congregate as a community. This megatrend, which many would say was born in Silicon Valley, has accelerated human evolution in an information-rich era. Technology is no longer a caste system or an exclusion mechanism; today technology and more specifically communication technology can be found in the pockets of over 5 billion people around the world, a figure that is still rapidly growing.

To understand where the digital revolution is taking us, it's important to reflect on where it came from. Prior to World War II, before mass adopted communication technology, the world was very personal. We knew the name of our bank manager and they knew us. Statistically, there was a strong chance your bank manager was invited to your wedding. But as corporations began to make aggressive attempts to globalise in the 1970s, they left behind the very thing that made business personal, that is genuine human interactions and relationships. Then as companies grew, financial pressures on margins and growth rates meant that modern organisations had to rethink how they interacted with and served the community.

There are firm indicators that suggest the 1990s was the most impersonal decade of the last century – indicating that things got progressively worse. This is most evident by talking to those in society that still remember the personal service they used to get from their bank manager. These people tend to be the ones that today still visit branches to update their passbook, like my mother.

Today many bank executives still cling to the notion that customers want branches. They are in part correct, but it's not really the branches that people want; it's the personal human interactions with people that actually know them and understand what they want. It's human nature to trust people we can associate with – people that demonstrate they understand us, care about our challenges and genuinely want to solve our problems. Very few digital businesses globally have managed to replace the *human* factor in digital interactions.

After we became comfortable with this new technology-enabled world, business and technology started to turn the corner and reconnect human nature, firstly as a means for competitive advantage, but increasingly as a core offering of a service. I draw your attention to the creation of Facebook, the birth of the smartphone and the rise of the digital native. These three parallel paths through time are the catalysts that drive the digital social economy. In isolation each of these trends is significant, transforming entire industries. But when you have a digitally native population frequently interacting and building communities through a technology that is never more than 3 metres away, the trends and the scale exponentially grow.

THE FACEBOOK GENERATION

The Facebook generation is one that is always on and always connected. They carry multiple forms of communication in telephony, instant messaging and email with them constantly. They expect higher levels of engagement and higher levels of demonstrated understanding by the service providers in their lives. This is a trend that stems from the era of context championed by the likes of Amazon, Spotify and Zappos; where unnecessary noise is removed from the engagement experience. Men aren't shown beauty salon deals; women in Australia aren't suggested services in the UK. What the user sees and experiences is relevant in that moment.

Businesses are customising their offering to match the profile and behaviour of their customers. As a result we see disciplines such as user experience design (or UX) becoming hugely influential success factors in many industries, including banking and financial services. Most of the cutting-edge banks today have dedicated user experience teams with coverage right across the organisation, across all customer's touch points, and these teams get involved in every single customer-facing initiative.

Why? Put simply, they are tasked with injecting the *human factor* into how banks build technology, which is something that's been missing from the banking technologies ever since the push for globalisation of organisations. UX teams champion ideas such as empathy, simplicity, experience and context – key factors in pleasing digital customers.

THE BIRTH OF THE SMARTPHONE

Probably the most important revolution I want to cover is that of mobility. Since the birth of the iPhone on 27 June 2007 (a mere six years ago) the power of mobile computing has taken off like a rocket. Prior to the iPhone very few businesses managed to build successful mobile experiences, primarily due to the complexity of building J2ME applications on Nokia devices that lacked frameworks, standards and controls. The iPhone meant that businesses of all sizes could develop on a common framework and deploy in a controlled ecosystem, simplifying the move into mobile.

The birth and growth of the smartphone market has to date been the single biggest impact of the proliferation of digital services globally. This growth will not slow until every person on the planet is carrying a smartphone, far exceeding the penetration of personal computers, laptops and even tablets.

THE RISE OF THE DIGITAL NATIVE

We've all heard terms like *Generation Y*, *Millennials* or *Generation M* – segments of classification used to pigeonhole people by their generation. In this passage I don't intend to debate, defend or define these labels. Just know that the only important factor we need to grasp from the labels is a trend that will change societal norms forever, this being the rise of a generation that only ever knew the digital world. These people don't associate with snail mail, landlines or the *Yellow Pages*. These people will grow up assuming everything is digital. It's why you see videos of two-year-old babies naturally navigating the iPad, but expressing frustration when interacting with a print magazine.

Gen Y is only the tip of the iceberg – they aren't even as pure digital as those born after them. But the behavioural tendencies, association frameworks and values of the generation give us a key insight into how a digital citizen might think, evaluate the world around them and act.

To date most traditional industries, including banks, have ignored the generational shift. Dismissing the generation as not profitable, or justifying ignorance through statements such as "Gen Y doesn't have money." But this is quickly changing. Many bankers of today neglect to realise that the birth year of a Gen Y is any date after 1980, meaning the generation is now lead by 33 year olds – just two years away from the marketer's sweet spot of 35 to 45.

Over the coming five years, the significance and value of this generation will rapidly accelerate. Not only because it will gain critical scale but also because this generation is an adoption leading indicator for all other generations. For example, while Gen Y was first to embrace Facebook, today the fastest growing demographic using the service is actually 55-year-old women. Initially this was because they jumped online to connect with their Gen Y children, but it is now increasingly because they are creating and engaging communities of their own interest(s).

DIGITAL VS REVOLUTION

The digital revolution is less about the digital aspect and more about the impact of the revolution. Purely by definition, the word revolution itself is very suggestive – change – but it also suggests change that has a community behind it. These are communities that prior to the internet and Facebook were virtually impossible to create on any meaningful scale without engaging large marketing and advertisement dollars spent in traditional media like print, television and radio. These traditional platforms only push a message on to the community and hope for conformity.

In the modern world, powered by platforms like Facebook, Twitter, blogs, Instagram and SnapChat, people of any interest or cause (no matter how esoteric) can find others with similar interests, despite geographic, socio-graphic, socioeconomic or any other barrier that would previously have stood between bonds forming these communities. If you're into underwater basket weaving, there is an online community for you.

The best example of a causal community is that of the Arab Spring in Egypt. This is a time in history that will forever be known as a turning point in the effectiveness of our modern connected society and should send shivers down the spine of any politician, business leader or brand. Prior to the Spring, Egypt had less than 15,000 Twitter accounts. Yet at the end of the two-week transformation some 22m people had joined and actively contributed to the community dialogue. This gained such strength in the nation that it was able to topple an autocratic government, one that had clung to power for decades through authority and force. I encourage anyone curious enough to Google the key statistics and trends from the Arab Spring – some of the most interesting case studies around digital community development come from that period.

I could reel off dozens of other examples of cause-based communities that scaled in the digital revolution. Ideas and opinions that became causes, causes that became communities, communities that became movements. They are not dissimilar to the end of slavery, women's rights, the Civil Rights Movement and more recently gay marriage, which are all cause-based communities that eventually gained enough scale and momentum to progress this cause into the mainstream. There are also dozens of these we have witnessed very publicly over the past five years, as communities get stronger and in leveraging the power of the connected economy. Instead let's focus our investigation on how community and causal scale impacts financial services.

IMPACT ON FINANCIAL SERVICES

Some of you will be aware of recent movements such as Occupy Wall Street and Occupy London, where digitally connected communities congregated to occupy prominent locations in major financial cities. These communities rallied around the idea that banks are bad, particularly after the events of the global financial crisis; a theme that had strong resonance with the world's population witnessing the systemic creation of predatory debt leveraged upon toxic debt, giving birth to systemic toxicity within the financial system (more commonly known as *subprime*).

Once brought to the attention of a few, opinions were formed amongst the members of a digitally connected society who shared their opinions, perspectives and outrage that the organisations society entrusted to manage monetary systems had prioritised commercial gains above systemic sustainability. An overwhelming number disagreed with this and a cause for coordination was created amongst those that stood against these "bad banks". This gave birth to an attempt at a revolution much in the same way that Egyptian people did not agree with their previous government, only without the ousting of a national leader.

The dictionary definition of the word revolution very much focuses on the replacement of government, but considering a lateral perspective one can see revolution in the digital world means an idea that has built critical mass to effect change. So could the digital generation create and drive a digital revolution purely based on banking reform? If so, what would it look like and how would it impact the incumbent financial services players? Are we suggesting a complete replacement of the old ways of banking is possible with the right cause?

In order to understand the future possibilities of the revolution within the financial sector, we need to take a closer look at the trends that are forming amongst the early adopter communities around the world. Ideas that at this point time may seem insignificant, or too small to have impact, have the DNA of what revolution could look like, giving us leading indicators of what our banking future may entail.

PRODUCT REVOLUTION

The first trend I draw your attention to comes from an unlikely direction, referencing the ever-growing adoption of prepaid products such as alternative checking accounts. Prepaid products have their origins in gift cards, travel cards and closed loop cash alternative systems such as Octopus, Oyster and EzLink, which over time have emerged as strong alternatives to cash. In the United States prepaid has gone beyond this, extending into markets traditionally owned and dominated by the banks.

One of the most prominent examples of the change is the success of Green Dot, a prepaid programme manager that has seen their general-purpose reloadable prepaid card go from zero to just under $700 billion in deposits over its short life. It continues to grow at roughly 26% per annum. The Green Dot Personalized Card is a prepaid Visa or debit MasterCard that you can use anywhere debit MasterCard or Visa debit cards are accepted worldwide. There's no line of credit associated with your card – it is just a prepaid debit card. Personalized Cards can be used at ATMs and can also be reloaded with more money. Your purchases and ATM withdrawals are debited from your card balance. Balance, spend and reload limits apply.

You might ask what is the attraction of this product. Why has it created such a shift in the mindset of consumers that a prepaid card is a viable alternative to opening a checking account? Put simply, the product is far more convenient to acquire and activate, more transparent on fees and embodies the credit avoidance behaviours of generation Y, i.e. no overdraft or credit interest. It's a simplified checking account for your everyday expenditure.

The psychological evaluation norms of the digital generation expect control and transparency. So the notion of credit interest and debit interest as line items on their statement create an element of distrust because they don't understand why or how these items occur. It looks like the bank is dipping their fingers into the pockets of its customers, even though for the majority of cheque account holders interest nets out with minimal impact on annual account balances.

A digital generation expects to be in control, all the time. So expect that the future of product in financial services will put the consumer in the driving seat through digital engagements.

DATA REVOLUTION

The second trend I want to look at is around data utilisation. The digital native has evolved to be more transparent with their data, to the point that they openly trust service providers to gain access to their data, such as your Facebook OpenGraph, Tweet history and transactional history. But this is only on the proviso that the data is used to derive value for the customer, in the way of context, value added insights, recommendations or peer comparison.

This is a far cry from their elders, who have been bred to be protective of personal data at all costs. The older generation is so paranoid that they attempt to delete cookies, opt out of email lists, and post minimal information on social network sites like Facebook, LinkedIn and Twitter. I'm not suggesting that the threats online are any less today, just that there is a significant mindset difference.

Instead of following in their elder's footsteps, the digital native appreciates and values a symbiotic exchange of value. The company wants your data in exchange for adding value to the experience, product or service for the consumer. By giving up this data, Facebook can make more accurate recommendations; ensure you only see relevant advertisements; or remove digital noise (a term commonly used for irrelevant content occupying screen space for a particular user). What results is a simpler, more targeted, value adding experience.

Compare this to the large majority of bank homepages and you'll observe a large disconnect between what is possible and what banks are doing. The homepage of most banks looks like a broadsheet newspaper – a desperate attempt to cram as much information as possible on high-value pages in a one-size-fits-all model of push communication. It's a frustrating experience when all you want to do is log on to internet banking.

MOBILE REVOLUTION

Many in the financial sector are reasonably familiar with the rapid rise of M-Pesa as the world's leading mobile payments system. It began as a project funded by the UK government Department for International Development (DFID) as a means for a more efficient collection of microfinance loan repayments. As the initial goal was quite humble, no one was prepared for the rapid growth. The system addressed a long-time systemic deficiency in the Kenyan financial system that excluded a majority of the population.

Success hasn't been limited to the developing economies. Mobile phones have been a large driving force behind the modality shift of consumer behaviour in banking around the globe. Consumers now expect access to their banking through their mobile phone, as a shift away from the internet and other traditional banking channels. Analytics leader comScore goes as far as to say that mobile banking is seeing 74% growth per annum and could see 50% of United States bank customers using mobile by 2016.[1]

With 5.9 billion mobile connections globally, mobile phones have far greater reach than any other distribution network in the world. By contrast, print newspaper only reaches 1.7 billion and the internet reaches 2.2 billion.[2] Mobile's reach goes beyond geographic and demographic barriers, showing that it doesn't matter if you work in a fish market in Kenya or a Bank in New York; there is equal access to a global network that connects the world's population.

The real power of mobile lies in the behaviour it empowers. Mobile is by its very nature personal – it's a device for an individual carried in a pocket, bag or hand. Increasingly people take their mobile phone everywhere with them. What makes mobile phones dramatically more personal is the nature of communications on the device. The mobile phone is seen as an individual's personal space – SMS, emails and messages on the device remain an individual's most sacred communications. Our secret corner of the hyper-connected world.

Not only is the mobile phone a personal space, it is a key service enabler. Our lives have shifted into the small screen of the mobile phone. Facebook has already seen roughly half its daily traffic shift to the mobile phone, while on Twitter 55% of traffic now comes from mobile devices.[3]

But why is this? What's behind the shift in behaviour? The answer is quite simple – the mobile phone is now used as a transportable medium, one that is equally powerful on the bus to the office, while waiting in a queue at the bank branch or while sitting in a park. It doesn't matter if you want to listen to music, read the news headlines or catch the latest episode of *American Idol*, all of these can be done on a transportable screen. It has become a behavioural norm in recent times that emails are sent from BlackBerrys or iPhones, mobile apps allow customers to buy coffee, shop for birthday gifts, or book a restaurant all while on the move, creating a population that is always plugged in.

But mobile has one more key trick up its sleeve that drives it as a channel of choice: contextualisation. Through the years of dot.com and social media, the idea of smarter user experience has developed concepts such as the *segment of one*, *contextualisation* and *relevance*. These concepts result in optimised experiences for the end user, but mobile takes that optimisation to a whole new level.

Suddenly time and location relevance can be applied, creating such unique experiences that they may only exist for a short amount of time at a specific location. Take for example the mobile user that opens Foursquare after finishing work for the day. Instantly they see a location-specific perspective on where their friends are now and where they can get a happy hour special. This shows the mobile device is not just a part of a virtual world, but also a guide in the physical world. A virtual world in which banks have very little engagement, or brand resonance.

COLLECTIVE REVOLUTION

Collective consumption is a new trend for our resource crunch times. Resources globally are under significant pressure to raise their utilisation rates, including property, land, money, food, etc. The idea of collective consumption is that it saves money, is good for the environment and brings communities together. Collective consumption refers to sharing, borrowing, swapping or renting equipment, resources and skills. Rather than buy a ladder or an expensive tool which you might only need once a month, why not borrow one? Don't splash out on a formal dress you are only going to wear once, rent one.

This trend has been embraced by the financial sector and person-to-person lending, crowd funding and collective buying have driven the rapid growth of businesses like Lending Club, AngelList and Groupon. Each has its own unique spin and position in market.

Lending Club is one of a dozen firms in the US, Europe and Australia whose model is to create a marketplace for loans similar to eBay's market for goods and services, with ordinary people lend money to other ordinary people via an online platform. Its success isn't isolated.

By 2016, peer-to-peer lenders in the US will be originating $20 billion in loans annually, according to Jason Jones, an organiser of the LendIt conference and partner at New York-based Disruption Credit, an investment firm focused on online lending. These figures don't include online loan programmes not available to retail investors, such as those of San Francisco-based Social Finance (SoFi), which may hand out as much as $1 billion in education loans in 2013.

AngelList is a US website for raising equity or debt investments for startups, leveraging the trend for crowd sourcing investment capital. Currently it's limited to accredited investors, but as the US's crowd sourcing regulations open up, platforms like AngelList could be the investment portfolios for Gen Y.

Groupon is the best known of the group buying platforms. Started in 2008, by October 2010 Groupon served more than 150 markets in North America and 100 markets in Europe, Asia and South America and had 35m registered users. While its success is subjective, it does create the precedence for strong group buying platforms.

ECOSYSTEMS ARE KEY

Like Kindle in books, iTunes in music and Netflix in movies, building the ecosystem is at the top of the list for key success factors. This may sound straightforward, but one needs to be aware this is not something you can buy, outsource or ignore. It's a constant journey of discovery, adaptation and refinement. It doesn't finish upon launch, nor does it finish within the first year. It is a journey that will engage you in the fascinating exploration of money and its utility within your market.

It involves understanding the various actors within the community, how and why they interact, where they interact and what the relationship is between them. Only with this level of understanding will the market opportunity for the digital revolution be obvious. This could be as simple as witnessing the amount of money that friends or family send between each other via trusted couriers, or how an individual goes about saving for a vacation. This is your secret source, engaging and understanding the world people live in, then finding the points in the ecosystem that could be better.

The world's startups already think like this. They diligently engage the market, working with them to innovate at rates that corporates struggle to comprehend. The insights derived from the engagement takes the guessing work out of building new products, services or businesses.

RECIPE FOR SUCCESS

Over my years of experience I have developed a framework to guide implementations to success in both developing and developed markets. The stages of this framework are: Engage, Penetrate, Accessibility, Control, Sustain & Learn, Re-plan, and Re-execute. Let's take a look at each step:

Ecosystem development model

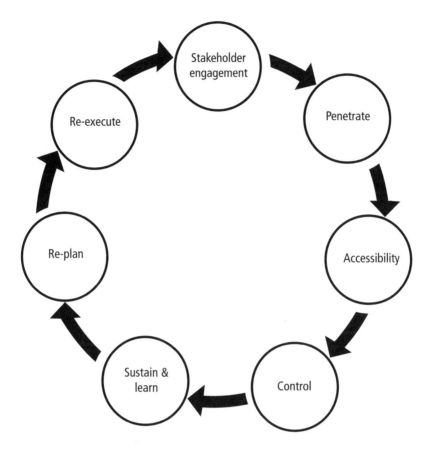

- **Engage**: First and foremost you must find a way to get amongst your target market. Spend time understanding their everyday needs, pressures, movements, etc. Find out how much cash they carry and why that amount. Where do they travel regularly to buy things, get services, or exchange money? Document everything you find, take photos, exchange contact details. These people will be key in your journey of market understanding and service refinement.

- **Penetrate**: With a clearer understanding of the market, document your theories or understanding on where you feel a service can penetrate the ecosystem. Remember that commerce and financial transactions already happen – you are just looking for gaps where you feel a service might enhance or benefit those involved. Start by listing just a dozen. This list is where you make a soft launch of the service. Get those people deeply engaged, because they will be your champions over time. These are purely assumptions for now.

- **Accessibility**: Now you have a few theories on getting into the ecosystem but you have to remember that once you convert transactions from money to the virtual economy, such as with mobile money, those individuals brave enough to be early adopters will need assurance that they can still get access to their money. There is no point trying to address the payday queues at a company if the only way they can get cash is to travel to a bank or ATM to make a withdrawal. The access needs to be within their current life and ecosystem. You already know how people's lives function from your findings at the Engage step.

- **Control**: While hyper-growth is fantastic, it also means you have to scale your service footprint to meet the demand, which creates a risk that you have poor customer experiences outside your existing field of service. Take Facebook for example – it executed a carefully controlled launch, one university at a time. During the initial phases of your launch you will learn ten-fold from your original market engagement findings. The ecosystem in which you activate needs to be readily accessible so you can quickly collect market feedback. Make sure you document this feedback, as it will be extremely valuable as you refine the service offering.

- **Sustain & Learn**: As the ecosystem organically grows, you need to maintain your engagement so that you may observe its growth patterns, behavioural usage, challenges, etc. Ongoing observation and documentation is required.

- **Re-plan**: Revisit the theories you had during the Penetrate phase and add to the list. No doubt the number of theories you now have will have doubled or even tripled. You need to link your findings in the field in a cyclical manner enabling a highly engaged feedback mechanism into your market planning, service planning and penetration plans. These will be key as you enter more and more ecosystems. Don't be afraid to remove the theories that didn't work, just don't forget why they didn't work.

- **Re-execute**: This is where the model completes the cycle. Go back and reengage, whether that is engaging a new ecosystem, or reengaging the same but broader community. You'll enter with an enhanced understanding, which will make you more observant and in tune with the community.

This may all seem fairly straightforward, but you'd be surprised how often companies looking to enter the digital frontier forget to engage the ecosystem and learn through a repeatable process. The process is scalable, so as your team size grows the process remains the same but with a greater power as you gain more and more perspectives on the market.

SUMMARY

Consumers in the digital world, particularly those born into a world that doesn't know or understand life before digital, think, act and evaluate the world very differently to their elders. They can build and create ideas that become causes – causes that can change entire industries, nations or products at such rapid rates the incumbents won't see it coming. This includes the highly regulated space of financial services.

Key trends to pay attention to are:

- Product revolution: Digital consumers want control, transparency and trust.

- Data revolution: If you are sitting on mountains of consumer data, make sure you are giving it back to them in the form of value adds, context and suggestions.

- Mobile revolution: Mobile cannot be ignored. It should be your first, second and third priority.

- Collective revolution: In the digital world consumers can and will connect directly to each other to solve problems, which may have you rethinking the role your organisation plays.

ENDNOTES

[1] www.mobilecommercedaily.com

[2] www.wan-press.org and www.internetworldstats.com/stats.htm

[3] www.readwriteweb.com/archives/facebook_mobile_usage_set_to_explode.php and therealtimereport.com/2011/10/21/mobile-devices-drive-more-than-half-of-traffic-to-twitter-and-pandora

RISK AND OPPORTUNITY IN THE DIGITAL REVOLUTION

BY ALAN BOYCE

ABOUT THE AUTHOR

Alan Boyce is managing director of Axonn Media Ltd, the biggest specialist content marketing company in the UK. Alan is a keen observer of technology trends and online behaviour, a passion which helps him and Axonn Media deliver highly successful content-led online campaigns for their clients.

INTRODUCTION: FROM BLACK MONDAY TO FLASH CRASH

ON 19 OCTOBER 1987 world financial markets crashed, with most major exchanges losing more than 20% of their value – and some shedding far more. The day quickly became known as Black Monday.

The blame was laid at the door of "programme trading", in which computers executed trades at high speeds automatically on the basis of data they were given and rules they followed blindly. It was thought that the feedback effects of computerised systems all selling at the first signs of a falling market led to the precipitous decline.

However, most markets recovered from Black Monday fairly quickly. The Dow Jones, which lost $500 billion of value that day, stood higher at the end of 1987 than it had at the start.

Twenty-three years later, on 6 May 2010, the Dow slumped by nearly 1000 points (9%) wiping $1 trillion in market capitalisation off the value of US businesses. Within an hour, most stocks had bounced back to their opening values. The Flash Crash, as it became known, was blamed on high-frequency trading (HFT) and algorithmic trading (AT), the direct technological descendents of the computer-based trading which was fingered as the culprit for Black Wednesday.

Digital technology thus has a long history of simultaneously attracting finance by the information advantages it promises and repelling it by the fear of control passing out of human hands. As in most other spheres where automation presents a double-edged sword, that attraction has continually triumphed over the repulsion.

PART 1: TECHNOLOGY AND FINANCE – FEAR AND OPPORTUNITY

Today, around 60% of trading in US financial markets is carried out by robots. In the UK, that figure is more like 30%. For better or worse, most major markets are now socio-technical systems featuring significant levels of human/robot and robot/robot activities as well as interhuman interactions.

In addition to carrying out activities autonomously, trading algorithms are also becoming adaptive – that is, computer programs are starting to design the next generation of computer programs. Their workings, both in terms of single operations and of aggregate market effects, may pass beyond human comprehension and control very soon. Finance is contemplating the central dilemma of a thousand science fiction stories: Should we stop this before the machines take over? *Can* we stop this?

But this is not just a story of bigger and faster computers bringing about a financial nirvana of perfect markets through perfect information. Today, the financial sector is confronted with a variety of specific technology trends, which offer opportunity and risk in equal measure. Moreover, in its contribution to globalisation and its ever-greater accessibility, IT is helping to transform the economic and political reality within which financial markets exist. Both finance and IT are, in turn, affected by what is going on in the rest of the world.

MORE INFORMATION, FASTER

The raw material of the finance industry is information. Information technology is fundamentally about the ability to process more and more information, faster and faster. Since the electric telegraph superseded the carrier pigeon, IT has been a central driver of efficiency in financial markets.

Today's digital revolution is accelerating that evolution at a logarithmic rate. Moore's law – the notion that computing power doubles every 18 to 24 months – appears to be proceeding unabated, but disturbing and unpredictable nonlinear dynamics are manifesting at the cutting edge. The superhuman speeds today's financial trading systems work at can, for example, allow dangerous feedback loops to multiply the effect of errors to catastrophic levels before anyone even notices.

In addition, there are significant new technological forces at play whose interactions with ever-greater processing power introduce even more uncertainty. The four most important of these are:

1. Cloud computing

2. Big data

3. Mobile

4. Social

I will look at these four forces in turn.

1. CLOUD COMPUTING

Cloud computing is making previously undreamt-of levels of processing power available to almost anyone, at a rapidly diminishing cost. The provision of on-demand virtual server capacity, located physically in massive, multi-tenanted data centres, is in some ways an updated version of 1960s utility computing. However, today's cloud provides many other kinds of applications – Software as a Service (SaaS) being the most well-known.

Until the cloud model emerged, technology-led approaches to financial analysis and trading were only possible for businesses and institutions able to maintain their own private infrastructure. Cloud is eliminating that barrier to entry by significantly reducing the cost of access to massive scale processing power. It is also creating opportunities for a whole host of software and middleware providers, encouraged by the European Union's MIFID Directive.

2. BIG DATA

The second phenomenon is *big data* – or rather, the growing ability of IT systems to analyse the enormous mass of unstructured, raw data; data that, until now, has been beyond the power of conventional databases to process.

It doesn't take much imagination to see what big data could do for the financial sector – in principle, nearly every financial problem is an information problem. And the data is out there: an April 2011 survey of American business by McKinsey found that in 15 out of 17 sectors examined, every single company stored more information than the 235 terabytes held by the US Library of Congress.

The big data revolution is about turning this mass of data into meaningful information and actionable knowledge. It has the capacity to transform the efficiency of business activity as well as the efficiency of financial systems.

3. MOBILE

The third and fourth drivers – mobile and social – are perhaps less obvious in their capacity to affect finance, but nonetheless they cannot be ignored. Each has the potential to send business practice along completely new trajectories, with significant consequences for the financial sector.

Mobile is a concept that encompasses more than just smartphones and tablets; it is the wholesale untethering of activity from location and the decentring of the IT department as the gatekeeper for technology.

Combined with the opening up of access to processing power offered by cloud, mobile has the capacity to end the dominance of traditional trading centres and recast the financial map of the world.

4. SOCIAL

Social media is the technology driver whose likely impact on financial markets is least apparent. It is hard to think how Facebook, for example, impinges on finance beyond the cautionary tale offered by its IPO.

Nevertheless, *social* – conceived of more broadly than particular platforms – is driving gamification, inter-organisational collaboration and crowdsourcing, the *permanent beta*, and more. The basis of the social web in a *need to share* as opposed to a *need to know* stance towards information could impact financial markets through deeper transformations of behavioural norms.

On the other hand, social media activity is providing a torrent of user data every day, which businesses ahead of the curve are exploiting – often in conjunction with big data techniques – to personalise their services and to model consumer behaviour. Some traders are already dependent on social media data in designing their strategies.

PART 2: RISKS OF THE DIGITAL REVOLUTION

Taken individually, each of the four drivers I identified has the capacity to transform finance. Together and in conjunction with other global trends, that capacity is exponentially greater – for better or for worse. I will begin by looking at some of the risks.

"Garbage in, garbage out," has long been a watchword of computer scientists. In March 2011, several Morningstar ETFs shed 98% of their value in minutes thanks to inaccurately keyed-in data (the so-called fat finger problem). The month before, errors in an oil futures trading algorithm sent volatility skyrocketing, shifting the oil price by $1 a barrel.

In both of these cases, the errors were spotted and the remedial action was taken to restore stability – by humans. But technology is reaching a point where humans may no longer be able to spot or unravel computer-generated problems.

Increasingly, financial systems are composed of a mixture of human and robot actors, with different relative proportions in different parts of the world and different markets. Experimental economics has long studied the interaction of human traders, while agent-based computational economics has looked at how robot systems behave together. There is relatively little scientific literature considering how mixed systems function and yet the global financial system as a whole and most of its significant constituent parts are just this kind of socio-technical hybrid.

Conventional financial modelling is therefore based on diminishingly relevant premises, and its predictive claims command less and less trust. Much more research is needed to understand how these new systems work, but whether it can be carried out before the technology moves to another level cannot be foreseen.

There are other technologically-induced reasons for fearing a loss of predictive capabilities too.

ROBOTS TALKING TO ROBOTS

Interacting HFT systems have the capacity to generate massive, market-overturning feedback effects (like the Flash Crash) at rates which leave humans able only to survey the bloody aftermath.

At the same time, supercharged by big data, automated systems can begin to do away with the need for human inputs and supervision. Machine learning is allowing trading algorithms to adapt in an evolutionary manner. Computers are generating and publishing financial data which other computers are receiving, processing and acting on. The behaviour of *robots talking to robots* may be extremely difficult to explain at the individual level, let alone at the macro level.

Already, markets are coming to expect the unexpected side-effects of automation. In the run-up to the Flash Crash of 2010, high levels of price volatility had been observed – but this was being discounted as normal. There is a risk that such normalisation of deviance could worsen future crises, by leading people to write-off warning signs – in high-speed, highly automated markets, prices themselves can cry wolf.

Without built-in circuit breakers and other ex-ante precautions (minimum tick sizes, notification of algorithms to the authorities, etc.) to stop them, runaway feedback loops pose an ever-greater risk to financial stability as speeds accelerate far beyond the rate of human thought. Most major exchanges have well-developed circuit breaker systems, although many refuse to publicise their trigger points.

Of course, at the velocities achieved by HFT, one could only be sure that a circuit breaker was working properly – in relative terms – long after the event. If it failed, it would be discovered far too late. And when the nonlinear dynamics that have been seen to emerge at the cutting edge of present technology are taken into account, the very scenarios circuit breakers are being designed to forestall are unknown, maybe unknowable.

INFORMATION SECURITY

This brings us to the enormous challenge of 21st century information security. Automated trading systems, interacting with one another and powered from remote, multi-tenanted locations, are not just more vulnerable to earthquakes, solar flares and other natural disasters than conventional financial markets. They are also critically vulnerable to cyber-attack.

The hackers have always been and remain one step ahead of those trying to stop them. Richard Clarke, former cyber security adviser to the US President, has said that "every major company in the United States has already been penetrated," while Defence Secretary Leon Panetta has acknowledged that all of the USA's critical infrastructure systems have been compromised. Nothing, it seems, is hacker-proof.

The sort of comprehensively-integrated global financial system operating more or less free of direct human oversight, which technological development is making a real possibility, is likely to prove an irresistible target for cyber-criminals – whether state-sponsored, motivated by love of money or just desirous of causing chaos.

From the bottom, the *bring your own device* trend being stimulated by developments in mobile represents a threat to information security, as does the spread of software procurement responsibility away from dedicated IT departments made possible by *appification* and SaaS.

Moreover, according to research from Deloitte, a growing number of hacker attacks are not accessing businesses directly but are coming through weak links in their trusted partner organisations.

THE REGULATORY CHALLENGE

Information security professionals may be hot on the heels of the hackers, but financial regulators are lagging much further behind their quarry. Computer-based trading has long been recognised as a potential source of market abuse – although, as a 2013 report by the UK Government Office for Science has shown, without much solid evidence. Nevertheless, the fear of abuse engendered by increasing automation erodes confidence, thus generating real economic effects.

There are two fundamental problems which any regulatory regime today has to confront.

Firstly, it has to be at least as sophisticated as the system it is trying to control, but as we have seen, the *system* has been radically expanded and is engaged in a technological arms race. Can a state authority hope to compete with the dynamism of the entire financial sector spurred on by the lure of profits? History suggests not.

Secondly, capital has never been more mobile, thanks to IT. The persistent threat of disinvestment deters governments from making their domestic financial regulatory frameworks more onerous, for fear of driving economic activity elsewhere. If capital moves from well-regulated markets to less well-regulated markets or unregulated dark pools, the risks of unstoppable feedback and inter-market contagion reappear.

It is hard to avoid the conclusion that a globalised financial system demands a more or less globalised financial regulatory system if it is to have a chance of containing the risks it throws up. That is a political challenge on an enormous scale. The speed at which the World Trade Organisation gets things done gives little cause for optimism in this respect.

POLARISATION

The final risk to consider is of a different order. Throughout the 20th century, there was widespread anxiety about the widening gulf between international finance and the real economy of manufacturing, jobs and people's livelihoods. We find ourselves, at the beginning of the 21st century, in a similar situation, with bankers publicly despised for creating a slump for the rest of us through their greedy machinations.

Whether he is correct or not, there are many who would agree instinctively with Paul Krugman when he said:

"It's hard to imagine a better illustration [of social uselessness] than high-frequency trading. The stock market is supposed to allocate capital to its most productive uses, for example by helping companies with good ideas raise money. But it's hard to see how traders who place their orders one-thirtieth of a second faster than anyone else do anything to improve that social function ... we've become a society in which the big bucks go to bad actors, a society that lavishly rewards those that make us poorer."

By accelerating financial markets to superhuman speeds and incentivising ever-more marginal trading, the digital revolution has the potential to strain the relationship between finance and the rest of society beyond breaking point. How such a showdown would end is impossible to foresee.

PART 3: DIGITAL POSSIBILITIES

It is, of course, entirely possible that none of these risks will come to pass. But the potential will always be there as technology ramps up the stakes of the game – in terms of both the spoils of success and the costs of failure.

There are three major areas of potential gain which I will focus on:

1. Market efficiency
2. Fairer global capital distribution
3. Choice and user experience

The first potential has been covered extensively already: in Part 1 from a technical point of view; in Part 2 from that of risk. Throughout, I have taken it more or less for granted that – in general – more information, faster is a good thing for financial markets.

If we stick with Krugman's aforementioned definition of the purpose of the stock market, it seems reasonable to assume that the digital revolution can improve the allocation of capital – by aiding price efficiency and removing barriers to price discovery. That in turn ought to lead to better returns for investors.

The cloud makes it possible for greater numbers of financial actors to access, process and act upon this data – while improvements in chipset design allow this to occur ever faster. Latency in cloud operations is still a barrier to perfect competition – HFT and other strategies that depend on outrunning competitors dealing with the same information deny the absolute cutting edge to smaller actors – but it can be assumed to be only a matter of time before this is dealt with.

Developments in computing power and the handling of big data have the potential to allow more accurate macro-modelling than is possible at the moment. If the lack of research into the functioning of mixed human/robot markets is addressed and effective safeguards from feedback and nonlinear dynamics are put in place, the kind of instability and volatility that has dogged financial markets since their inception could be contained.

It is probably naive to imagine that computers can eliminate all uncertainty from finance and that markets can be truly perfected by information handling – as Stiglitz and Grossman showed in 1980 with the notion of the *price paradox*. Moreover, there is no definite technical limit to the quantity of data that could be taken into consideration and the speed at which it could be analysed.

If all actors are racing to take advantage of one another by being bigger and faster, the rate of technological advance and the distribution of new knowledge would have to be taken into consideration. In particular, the absence of shared standards for software and data represent a significant barrier to complete transparency between financial actors at the present time. Of course, it seems reasonable to suggest that even if markets may never reach a state of perfection, there is plenty of room for improvement still to be achieved.

With profits to be made on the margins, by outpacing or outprocessing rivals, it is likely that financial actors will be more secretive with their data and with their algorithms in defence of their competitive advantages. However, there is an alternative scenario which is being offered up by social.

NEED TO KNOW VERSUS NEED TO SHARE

Many spheres of online life are witnessing a revolution of collaboration. Barclaycard recently crowdsourced the features for a new credit card from its customers, enabling them to offer a highly attractive product with minimal R&D. Kaggle is a platform for big data analytics, which encourages volunteers to put their skills to the test on real-world questions.

Trading houses are already scouring social media networks for the mass of unstructured data about behaviour they offer. Kickstarter encourages individuals to become venture capitalists (of sorts) on projects they care about.

There is, at large in the world, a force urging that *data wants to be free* and its proponents are often highly technically literate, even evangelical. The counterforce, of course, has the backing of corporate weight and the more or less tacit endorsement of state authority.

The digital revolution, however, is more than just a technological revolution – it gets a great deal of its force from the fervour, energy and commitment of its adherents, many of whom display (even if they do not espouse) libertarian tendencies. Jeff Bezos' acquisition of the *Washington Post* perhaps offers a synecdoche of this struggle. Or maybe not – maybe big web companies are really the same as big pre-web companies at heart.

GLOBAL JUSTICE, YOUR PREFERENCES

Cloud and mobile technology, in turn, have the capacity to challenge the hegemony of traditional financial centres. Infrastructure problems have long handicapped the development of financial sectors in the developing world – as well as the self-interest of the West. The virtualisation permitted by these new technologies removes that major barrier. At a time when capital is flooding into previously-neglected parts of the world, such as Africa and Asia, technology trends present the prospect of a financial renaissance.

When everything is processed in a remote data centre and executed via the internet, what intrinsic advantages will there be to listing in London or New York? Virtual trading networks may be able to spring up, taking advantage of a lack of jurisdictional clarity, supplanting the old, bricks and mortar exchanges. Of course, there are skills barriers and issues of property rights and even the rule of law to be taken into consideration – but the benefits are potentially enormous.

Finally, at the individual level, technology has the potential to transform how we interact with financial services. Barclaycard's crowdsourcing efforts have already been mentioned. British American Express users can sync their card use with FourSquare, to take up location-based offers. Spanish bank BBVA's website has an online assistant to help its customers carry out their online banking.

Many financial outlets are already following the lead of Amazon, Starbucks and other pioneers of personalisation to learn about their customers and offer them more engaging experiences.

PART 4: TECHNOLOGY, FINANCE AND GEOPOLITICS

Neither finance nor IT exist singly or jointly in a vacuum. There are other forces at work in the world today which pose significant challenges to both, and which have the potential to reroute their direction of travel.

Not everyone in the world is content to see the financial system continue working in the way it historically has, and to the benefit of those it has historically rewarded. There have always been states that have attempted to affect financial markets with their own brands of economic nationalism, but none has ever perhaps posed quite such a challenge to the paradigm of free market Western finance capitalism as China.

The rise of China cannot be separated from the digital revolution – they are intrinsic parts of one another's context. China manufactures most of the world's IT hardware – it is perhaps as responsible as the cloud for the democratisation of access to computing power through its role in lowering costs. Chinese researchers have produced more academic papers in computer science and related subjects than any other country since 2009.

The Chinese state uses finance and investment as instruments of political power. Far more than other states – most of which are either laissez faire by conviction or incapable of making much of a difference – it is an actor and a disruptor in markets. One need only look at China's acquisition of US sovereign debt and the persistent over-valuation of the Yuan to see this. Chinese investment in Asia and Africa is changing the economic face of those continents, just as IT is presenting them with new opportunities. Along with Russia, it also stands accused of using cyberwarfare for politico-economic gain.

China's relative economic success compared to the sluggish and sclerotic progress of the democratic nations also poses profound questions about whether economic liberalism always implies political liberalism.

As well as state actors, the globally automated financial system must contend with rogue non-state actors – so-called *hacktivists*, motivated not by financial gain but by political conviction. Already, one can see the battle lines drawn out; over the WikiLeaks affair, Edward Snowden and Project Prism, and more. We have witnessed how theoretically vulnerable an integrated, automated global financial system could be to hackers. The idea has even entered the popular culture mainstream – witness supervillain Bane's laptop-powered attack on the Gotham City Stock Exchange in 2012's movie *The Dark Knight Rises*.

The flipside of this peril is the progress of cyber-utopians in making their dreams a reality. Bitcoin and other wholly digital currencies are being taken increasingly seriously, offering a way for finance to transcend the physical world. In the summer of 2013, German financial authorities, for example, acknowledged bitcoin as a financial instrument, while the US Senate is inquiring into it and other virtual currencies.

These trends magnify and frame the potentialities of the digital revolution for finance. It is, of course, impossible to say which tendencies will prevail and which will be the *never-weres* we all look back and laugh about in years to come. Uncertainty will definitely remain a *buy* commodity for the foreseeable future. That is as close to a sure thing as you can get.

PREPARING FOR DIGITAL DISASTER – INVISIBLE RISKS WITH CATASTROPHIC IMPLICATIONS

BY JOHN DUNCALF AND DAVID COVERDALE

ABOUT THE AUTHORS

John Duncalf is a Chartered Insurance Practitioner with over 50 years working experience of the insurance sector and industry. He has spent the last 20 years specialising in the corporate insurance requirements of UK financial institutions.

David Coverdale is a consultant in business continuity and risk management and is owner of BCP4me continuity management software. His career of 33 years includes insurance, TQM, process engineering and executive positions in Xerox, Pace and Sharp Electronics. Today David provides risk and continuity services to major insurers, brokers and their clients.
www.bcp4me.co.uk

INTRODUCTION

IN THE DIGITAL age, are businesses, insurance brokers and insurance companies walking blind into the perfect storm? Unrecognised risks, denial, ignorance and a lack of solutions to threats from loss of data, information and reputation abound for the unprepared.

For the purposes of corporate insurances, can you be certain that all your appropriate risk exposures have been fully identified, prioritised, properly insured and, essentially, complemented by a tested disaster recovery and business continuity plan? If not, then your business could come to a sudden and unexpected termination!

THE CHANGING FACE OF BUSINESS CRIME

There is an ever-increasing number of alarming reports of cyber/digital losses and security breeches – as witnessed by such news stories as "British defence giant hit by wave of cyber attacks". Another recent headline referred to £27 billion of cyber/digital losses per annum and the UK business sector having the worst protection against such events globally. It has been further reported that during 2012 nearly every industry and type of data was involved in a breach of some kind.

British Intelligence has stated that Britain is under daily attack in cyberspace, seeing some 70 sophisticated cyber espionage operations a month against government and industry. A GCHQ director has said that business secrets are "being stolen on an industrial scale".

Today's criminal is not so likely to physically break and enter your business premises and steal your assets as they are to be a web wizard, or a devious computer programmer, operating in a remote part of the world. It is a change from the hooded villain with a jemmy to a technically savvy industry of organised crime. The dynamics of crime, which can destroy balance sheets at a stroke, have changed beyond all recognition. Today's most damaging threats are most certainly led by cyber/digital risks.

The two greatest concerns of CIOs and CTOs in business today are security of information within the business and power supply, but even here there is an assumption that technical solutions will be sufficient to protect the business, whereas the fallout on reputation, standing and future revenues may lie outside their brief.

Historically the template used in the insurance sector for initially assessing risk exposures to be insured was to ask what the law says must be insured, what contractual liabilities are required to be insured and what other risks are commercially prudent to insure. However, far too frequently the insurances effected were not tested with forward or lateral thinking or constantly subjected to "What if?" scenarios beyond the boundaries of the business.

What if:

- the premises next door burnt down overnight?
- there is a prolonged prevention of access to our premises?
- our major supplier or customer goes out of business?
- our delivery driver fails to tell us that he has been banned from driving and is subsequently involved in a fatal accident caused by his negligence whilst driving on behalf of our business?

These are all potentially damaging scenarios, but today the far more serious "What ifs?" are likely to be as follows. What if:

- we are subjected to cyber extortion?
- our IT system fails?
- a sacked employee stole our data prior to dismissal?
- we are using unlicensed content in our social media marketing strategy?
- our intellectual property is stolen or we are accused of stealing such from another?

Today every aspect of business, and life as a whole, is dominated by IT – finance, purchasing, socialising, etc. – so it is inevitable that digital information is now the most valuable target for criminals, whether they are attacking your firm with an aim in mind or whether they simply want to be malicious and cause damage.

Essential risks to be considered in this space include:

- computer virus
- employee error or malicious action
- internal and external attacks
- virus transmission
- defamation, libel, slander
- privacy and plagiarism
- website and e-commerce liabilities
- internet content liability
- network security liability
- crisis management
- intellectual property
- power surge/failure

- theft
- physical damage
- natural disaster

RISK TO REPUTATION

Whereas the event of any of the above, either singularly or collectively, can be damaging enough it is the further knock-on effect of damage to reputation – reputational risk – which is the most critical of all. The Federal Reserve of the US has defined reputational risk as the potential that negative publicity regarding an institution's business practices, whether true or not, will cause a decline in the customer base, costly litigation or revenue reductions. It is essential that any disaster recovery plan factors in crisis management and the protection of reputation. In reality, a plan within a plan.

Reputational risk correlates with ever-intense public scrutiny, as evidenced by financial institutions being scrutinised for their tax structures; supermarkets and food suppliers criticised over horsemeat contamination; and fashion retailers questioned for selling goods manufactured in unacceptable working conditions in the developing world.

Today, especially via social media, a company's reputation can be seriously damaged in hours. Reputation is difficult to manage and is increasingly at risk, particularly from globalisation, regulation and the media. It is far too easy to underestimate the challenges of crisis management but businesses must improve in measuring and managing external perceptions. It is essential to mitigate any damage early and also to prevent reputational risk events from happening in the first place.

INSURANCE INDUSTRY AND BUSINESSES NEED TO ADAPT

In 1999 Bill Gates defined the fundamental change in global business in the new century as "business at the speed of thought". All aspects of business are accelerated by the digital revolution and the exponential use of technology, data, communications and applications. But with this acceleration comes the proportionately greater consequence of system failure, attacks and system breaches.

Despite the fact that today's cyber/digital risk exposures effectively took their rise from the computerisation of business in the mid-1980s, the insurance sector, with some exceptions, has been woefully slow to adapt to the reality of today's needs. Many insurers have been resistant to change and many brokers have not trained their staff to lead the appropriate and necessary dialogue with their clients.

All too frequently insurances are arranged by dialogue between the broker and the client executive responsible for insurances when, in fact, the process should embrace all operational managers and, in this context, especially the IT manager. Even then some IT managers, invariably fearing internal censorship, can be hugely resistant to helping identify those risks which essentially need to be insured or weaknesses which need to be rectified.

As previously inferred, to be totally effective every corporate insurance portfolio must be complemented by a tested disaster recovery and business continuity plan. As this essentially involves every operational area and manager in the business, to gather the required level of detail a business should undertake a full business impact assessment – this is the most effective means of identifying and prioritising the impacts, dependencies and risk exposures, including those which need to be insured.

Business needs to look less at the risk of an interruption or loss of functionality and more at the impact of such an occurrence. Impacts are more far-reaching and even terminal when resulting in loss of reputation and revenue. Insurance of the physical is still a requirement, but with more workspace alternatives, new working methods and remote access, it is risks to data and communications which may be more critical. The consideration should be less about "What if?" and more about "What next?"

Is it not the case that our perception of major brands suffering a loss of data plummets immediately and that there is almost nothing they can do to restore it? Consider the damage to the NatWest brand and share value following the payroll malfunction in 2012. Is the insurance industry prepared for a shift away from the physical and towards protection against data loss and cyber theft, and paying out against the potential value of reputational impact? Hark back to the disastrous underwriting of the risk of advancements in IT in the 1980s, which nearly bankrupted at least one major Lloyd's syndicate at the time.

BUSINESS IMPACT ASSESSMENT

Businesses need to undertake a granular business impact assessment (BIA) to fully understand each activity, its impact on the business, and how each depends on IT, data, systems and communications. There is a tendency to consider business continuity purely as disaster recovery within IT – in other words to ensure the data is routinely backed up. But this simplistic and convenient approach is out of date, on the one hand creating a false sense of security with an untested and unrestored set of data, or on the other, an over-provision of replicated data and systems which most activities in the business may not need.

There are templates and guidelines on business impact assessments available on the web, or through bodies such as the BSI, BCI, www.gov.uk and many consultancies, which follow a broadly similar process of interrogation. Some enlightened brokers and insurers are offering this capability to their clients to support the assessment of risk, but also as the basis of forming the business continuity plan (BCP).

One approach to energise the business impact assessment and to engage executives in the findings is to create a one-page pictorial view of the impacts on the business, colour-coding areas of greatest concern and where breaches of Service Level Agreement, contract or compliance may be a risk. Such a heat map captures the impact of losing a specific activity – such as *operations* – by measuring the effect on reputation, revenue and customers, adding them together, and multiplying by the likelihood of disruption.

So rather than the traditional 5 x 5 measurement of risk where the scores are very similar, this method provides a range from 5 to a maximum 75, and clearly identifies the impacts and priorities which would effect the business. The dependencies on IT and non-IT resources are then captured and the time needed for the restoration of each which feed into the continuity plan.

This heat map was developed by BCP4me.net and is used by clients of all sizes to demonstrate the critical areas of impact across the business. Ideally a degree of challenge and external "what about..." questioning adds value to the process, and cuts through internal politics and inertia. An example of such a pictorial heat map is shown in Figure 1.

Figure 1 – example business impact assessment heat map

Sample Business Impact Assessment - Heat Map: Company: XYZ. Date: 00/00/00 Owner: TBA

Key function	Peak Times	Impact Hours	R	C	Cr	L	Impact Score	RTO hours	Contract	SLA	Mitigation	Actions
							Assessment of impacts			Recovery and Mitigation		
Finance	Monthly	0	4	3	4	4	44	4	No	Yes	Required	
Production	Hourly	4	3	5	5	3	39	12	Yes	Yes	Required	
Marketing	Qtrly	24	2	3	3	2	16	72	No	No	Acceptable	
Sales	Monthly	48	3	4	4	2	22	72	Yes	No	Acceptable	
Technical	Daily	24	4	5	5	3	42	48	Yes	Yes	Required	
I.T.	Hourly	2	5	4	5	4	56	2	Yes	Yes	Required	
Management	Daily	12	2	2	3	3	21	4	No	No	Acceptable	
Etc...												

Key: R=Reputation; C=Customers; Cr=Criticality; L=Likelihood   (displays in colour)

With a clear understanding of the dependence on IT, data and recovery times – by activity – specific security, back up, replication and retrieval can be planned, and appropriate measures and cost applied.

INFORMATION SECURITY

Where the importance of information and data is recognised, there are other considerations for the executive and insurer. More companies are turning to offsite, cloud or third-party management of their IT and storage of data. In this case, who is the data and process owner? Where does the responsibility lie, both for the safe storage and management of the information, and more importantly, for the impact of a breach? Can you sue the cloud? Do you know where the cloud is ultimately owned and/or located? Is it in a truly safe and legal environment?

Companies who seek and adopt the ISO27001 Standard on Information Security deserve concessions from the insurer, provided they can evidence buy-in and engagement in all aspects of the protection and good management of data. However, there does not yet appear to be a correlation between holders of Standards and a clean bill of health at an operational level.

With the growth in convenience IT, we are pressed into accepting new technology and applications without being made aware of the underlying consequences of our actions. The terms and conditions in end-user contracts emanating from US providers should give corporate lawyers sleepless nights. For example, Google Mail gives Google the right to inspect, intervene on the basis of, or reuse any information sent or received using their platform.

In relation to general insurance, many policies exclude the US and make this an additional provision, based on the higher impacts of litigation in the US. However, when it comes to data stored and managed in the US, are companies and their insurers aware of the consequences and legal issues herein, or even that their data is stored in the US?

Businesses and insurers need to challenge the policy, procedures and behaviours in each client with regard to information security to raise awareness and drive compliance to reduce the risk of data loss.

ACTION-ORIENTED CONTINUITY PLAN

Having undertaken the business impact assessment and formed a clear understanding of recovery times, resources and dependencies, a clear action-oriented continuity plan can be developed. It is critical that the timeframes identified in the assessment are built into the plan. As a crisis develops, with new media and technology, the management of communications and reputation are pushed to the fore.

Where plans exist they can often be little more than a collection of policies, documents and potential contacts, internal and external. They tend to lack actions to facilitate the handling of the incident, the management of communications and the recovery of the business. To be effective, the plan needs to set out the detailed activities to achieve the requirements and timings identified in the BIA, with each task assigned, timed and tracked to ensure progress.

How might insurance help a business in the early hours of an incident when the situation, perhaps a breach of private data, becomes public, and the consequences are debated on Twitter and Facebook? Each passing tweet and comment may deepen the crisis and increase the impact on the business and its loss. Might a concerted media campaign cause the share price to fall? How is this addressed in the plan?

The management team in a business needs to be fully engaged in their business continuity programme, prompting involvement across the business and preparing for possible scenarios. To date, such consideration of scenarios will generally look at the physical rather than the impact of a major data loss or system breach. In this new cyber world, planning and undertaking exercises based on data loss, theft and cyber attack are perhaps more important than restoration following a fire.

Consider also the move towards online transactions to bolster sales and reduce costs. This looks so attractive, until a full penetration test shows that by placing an online order, with some fairly basic knowledge of website construction access can be gained to the data and file structure behind the web pages. Businesses which trade on the web should be pressed to demonstrate that they have completed full penetration tests.

A further thought with the move to ever more global and shorter supply chains is where the responsibility for loss lies. Companies not only need to look into their own resilience and continuity, but should insist on their suppliers and partners being as resilient and able to meet their Service Level Agreements. When this comes to protection of data and IT, it further complicates the role of insurance up and down the supply chain.

BEGINNING THE SHAKE UP

All this considered, where does an organisation start to address the risks created by what is a seismic shift in technology? A recent report from Deloitte perhaps sheds light on why the UK business sector is seen as having the worst protection against cyber/digital attacks globally. Their study of 86 financial institutions showed only incremental progress since a similar study two years ago and stated that insurers, banks and asset managers have shown slow progress in tying executive pay to risk and improving data to spot emerging dangers.

Additionally only 55% of those considered in the study included risk management in performance goals and compensation for senior managers. Risk management was even less of a priority for staff and middle managers with only a third of businesses reporting that this was factored into compensation decisions.

As this poor performance persists despite substantial increases in risk management spending, it suggests that risk is not fully embedded in the very culture of business. For any culture to be effective it has to be totally embraced at every level, starting at the top and supported throughout with knowledge, understanding and openness.

Therefore a first move could be the appointment of a non-executive with the necessary knowledge and experience to disrupt the comfort zone which might exist anywhere in the organisation with regards to data, IT and reputational impact. Insurers and brokers would do well to broaden the scope of their client appraisal, and to train their executives on impact assessment and non-physical risks.

IT managers should provide evidence of good practice, resilience and testing to the executive, but in a form and language understood by all to provide assurance and confidence to the board and stakeholders.

Insurers might consider the need for a more specific range of products based on cyber loss and reputational impact and offer new markets to the brokers for their clients to select as this change accelerates.

Businesses should regularly review their approach to business continuity planning, both physical and non-physical, and consider that the likelihood of data breach or loss is far greater than the risk of fire and the impact potentially much greater. Business continuity is not a problem, it is a process. However, when it is not a process, then it becomes a problem.

NEXT GENERATION HEDGE FUNDS

BY DOMINIC HEYDEN, ALEXANDER SURMINSKI AND PHILIPP DOERING

ABOUT THE AUTHORS

As the architect of ayondo's technology from the ground up, Dominic Heyden is responsible for ensuring a smooth running and technical vision for ayondo's IT and its operations. Through and through a child of the internet, he wrote his first lines of code at the age of six and has over 15 years of experience in the development and scaling of web applications. In addition, he gained several years of experience in international IT consulting and project management, most recently at one of the world's leading enterprise search vendors.

Alex Surminski is responsible for marketing, advertising and PR, as well as HR, customer and affiliate management. As a marketing crack he brings years of experience to ayondo, especially from the financial industry which he gained at companies such as ABN AMRO Bank, Royal Bank of Scotland, OnVista Bank and EFG Financial. Alex is a graduate in business administration from the University of Cologne.

Philipp Doering is part of the ayondo team. He studied management and economics at the University of Bochum with a focus on finance and quantitative analysis. Besides his studies he did several internships and worked as a student assistant at the chair of banking and finance, where he inter alia carried out research on providing incentives to portfolio managers.

INTRODUCTION

OVER THE PAST decade hedge funds have achieved spectacular growth. Despite the setback of the financial crisis in 2008, assets under management resumed to reach new all-time highs in 2012.[1] However, the financial crisis and subsequent knock-on events related to hedge funds, such as the revelation of the Madoff Ponzi scheme, cast a dark shadow on the industry and inspired debates about the tightening of regulative guidelines. This article draws parallels between hedge funds and the opportunities provided by *social trading* and presents the benefits of the latter.

The term *social trading* can be defined as an exchange of trading signals within specialised social networks. The two main parties exchanging signals in social trading are *traders* and *followers*. Traders publicise their trading signals, which were placed either in their virtual or real money trading accounts, to which followers can subscribe to. From a wealth of traders, followers can compile a trader portfolio which can then be executed in a brokerage account.

Although there are social trading platforms which allow followers to manually intervene or reject signals, a fully automated and unsupervised mirroring of the traders' signals in the followers' accounts without their confirmation prevails. The advantage of the automatic replication of trading signals is that they are copied without considerable delay (and thus without considerable slippage). Social trading platforms serve as an intermediary between traders and followers, providing the technical framework as well as the *rules of the game*.[2]

CHARACTERISATION OF HEDGE FUNDS

Hedge funds are collective investment schemes that invest private capital speculatively in order to maximise enhancement in value.[3] The first hedge fund in history is credited to have been founded by A.W. Jones in 1949. He referred to this as a "hedge*d* fund" instead of hedge fund, as he believed that hedging against a downside risk by shorting the market was the key characteristic of what he did in comparison to mutual funds.

Nowadays, the notion that such funds generally hedge their positions may not be valid anymore.[4] In fact, they do not face many constraints regarding their investment activities and use a variety of different strategies. Although an exact classification is limited due to permanent changes, a common approach to distinguish between hedge fund strategies is to focus on their exposure towards systematic risk.

Market neutral funds are characterised by beta close to zero, whereas *directional funds* place bets on market movements so they usually have a high correlation with the overall market return.[5]

Besides various types of strategies there are other more fundamental characteristics with regard to hedge funds. In contrast to mutual funds they are allowed to open long as well as short positions in order to generate *absolute return* and usually do so by leveraging, borrowing funds or using derivatives. In addition, orientating themselves towards investors classified as professional, such as institutional investors or high net-worth individuals, they only face minimal regulative boundaries.[6] In fact, in many parts of the world it is forbidden to sell hedge fund shares to retail investors. While in the United States this is enforced by the Securities Act of 1933, in Germany it is an integral part of the draft law to implement the AIFM-Directive[7] and is therefore a work in progress.

Another key characteristic is the illiquidity of hedge fund shares due to lock-up agreements, which often means they can only be traded on a weekly or monthly basis. Furthermore, hedge funds almost always raise performance fees.[8] Common remuneration schemes are the "two-twenty rule", meaning the fund charges 2% per annum on the assets under management and 20% on realised profits or performance fees that are to be paid if the fund exceeds a historical peak in value (known as a *high watermark*).

COMPARISON BETWEEN SOCIAL TRADING AND HEDGE FUNDS

Some basic similarities can be identified when realigning the above-mentioned hedge fund characteristics and trying to apply them to social traders:

- **Absolute return and leveraged trading**: As most social trading platforms mainly offer derivatives trading by contracts for difference (CFD), traders can open leveraged positions on the long or short side which are then replicated in follower accounts. CFD trading involves the deposit of a margin as a fraction of the notional value, which means the holder of a CFD contract disproportionally participates in the movements of the underlying asset. Currently, social trading platforms offer equity indices and major forex pairs as well as certain commodities, precious metals and equities as underlyings. Though the platforms provide traders with a limited investment universe compared to hedge fund managers, they do provide an investment structure similar to hedge funds.

- **Limited to professional investors**: Principally, following traders via social trading is not limited to a certain type of investor.

- **Regulation**: Although not directly facing governmental regulation, traders sharing their transactions via social trading are subject to legal and technical restrictions provided by the platform (e.g. accepting the general terms and conditions).

- **Liquidity (lock-up agreements and limited tradability)**: Followers as signal receivers are usually not confronted with any liquidity restrictions at all.

- **Compensation scheme**: Until now, no predominant compensation scheme for traders has emerged. This is one point where current social trading platforms tend to differ – while some pay performance-based fees including a high watermark, others offer a strictly asset-based remuneration. In fact, social trading offers opportunities for compensation schemes exceeding those possible for hedge funds. As an example, ayondo recently introduced a compensation scheme that provides traders with a two-fold incentive by automatically classifying traders in conjunction with a five-step trading career. Traders can reach each career level upon fulfilling pre-determined rules on selected return and risk measures over a certain period. Since it makes sense to assume that the number of followers will increase due to the trader's improving risk-adjusted returns (traders are displayed in rankings lists so this can be seen), traders are induced to trade well in order to increase their compensation by gaining more followers. They are also encouraged to sustain a good track record by the attractive possibility of being upgraded and increasing their share of generated volume per trade. As a knock-on effect, the idea of stepped career levels to reach a final goal (the *institutional level* of traders) has a binding effect on the trader.

Moreover, trader strategies within social trading can be classified as market neutral as their betas are close to zero. In a nutshell, social trading gives investors the opportunity to invest in advanced, market-neutral, small-money hedge funds.[9]

But what are the advantages in detail?

DETAILED ANALYSIS OF SOCIAL TRADING ADVANTAGES

As explained above, there are some similarities between social trading and hedge funds, but also some areas where social trading has advantages. When it comes to transparency and liquidity especially, social trading offers a number of additional benefits.

REGULATION AND TRANSPARENCY

Hedge funds do not face strong regulation since they are allowed to raise capital only in non-public offerings from investors strictly classified as professional. In contrast to mutual funds, they are not obliged to report their activities to third parties in detail and in fact some funds have low transparency even to investors.[10]

In order to acquire additional investors, hedge funds may decide to report certain information to consolidated databases voluntarily.[11] Usually measures like return, net asset value, investment style, fees and inception dates are published. However, a major part of the data available in these databases is self-compiled and not scrutinised by third parties.

In a study on two major databases for hedge fund reporting, it was found that a large number of funds that voluntarily provided information had significant discrepancies within their reports and 5% of the reported return and net asset value measures were dramatically different.[12] Due to these deviations, potential investors tend to be forced to do their own research; the measures provided by such databases at best serve as a rough guidance.[13]

On the contrary, social trading platforms offer standardised and verified real-time information on trader performances. Depending on the platform, publicly displayed benchmarks are not limited to popular return and risk metrics like risk-adjusted returns or the maximum drawdown. Platforms like ayondo also publish benchmarks like asset allocation, proportion of winning trades and periods, as well as various other measures and advanced visualisations. Nonetheless, probably the most important added value (compared to most classic hedge funds) is the public listing of the entire transaction history for every trader on the platform. As an example, ayondo publicises the complete transaction histories on the platform even to non-registered visitors. Based on this level of total transparency, every potential investor has the opportunity to do his or her own individual analysis as all the information is publicly available, free of charge.

Social trading platforms are more than one step ahead in this regard: they utilise the possibilities of the internet in order to provide full transparency to investors and the public in general. This may help retail as well as professional investors in making rational decisions and leads to a certain self-regulation. Hedge funds for the most part are characterised by a low transparency and would be well advised to improve their reporting.

LIQUIDITY

Investing in hedge funds generally revolves around buying shares, either by providing equity during fund raising stages or by purchasing shares from previous shareholders on the secondary market. One of the key characteristics of equity is permanence – the only opportunity of disinvesting is to sell shares, which is solely possible when the demand is there. Especially when it comes to hedge funds, investors are tied to lock-up agreements and the ability of trading the shares is often limited to certain dates. Additionally, the sale of shares may incur transaction fees.

In the context of social trading, followers do not face any liquidity issues at all. They can stop following the traders allocated in their portfolio at any time with just a single click and without any considerable delay. Followers of social trading can reassemble their portfolio of traders at any moment. Additionally, no fees arise for replacing a subscribed trader. In fact, social trading platforms such as ayondo offer features like loss protection or the possibility of halting trade execution in order to utilise the liquidity advantage of replicating trades. That is to say, followers don't have to sell their shares. They can simply stop the process of having trades replicated in their account and they aren't restricted by demand, or lack of demand.

ACCESSIBILITY AND AUTONOMY

The prerequisite for selling hedge fund shares is to first own them. This is bound to certain criteria. In the US, hedge funds are only allowed to raise capital in non-public offerings from high net-worth individuals with a certain income or accredited investors which are defined by the Securities Act of 1933. Within the EU, Germany recently decided to forbid selling alternative investment funds (AIF) to retail investors. Hedge funds are classified as AIF. Within the draft law[14] to transpose the AIFM directive[15], the German parliament agreed upon privileging professional and semi-professional investors. To put it simply, semi-professionals are high net-worth individuals. Furthermore, it is typical for hedge funds to stop accepting additional funds after they have raised a target amount of capital.

For retail investors, the only opportunity to invest in hedge funds is by purchasing special clone exchange traded funds (ETFs). In general, there are three ways for ETF managers to provide hedge fund-like exposure: by imitating a hedge fund index using a *beta replication strategy*; by attempting to track certain portfolio allocations of hedge funds; or by investing directly in the hedge funds themselves. Each of these ways face individual issues:

- **Hedge funds index replication**: A major strategy to mimic hedge fund returns is to track a hedge funds index. Whereas various studies by investment banks and academic research papers indicate that attempting alpha is a zero-sum game overall[16], ETFs focus on replicating the beta typical for the sector. They track the historical hedge fund returns relative to the market return and utilise this data to estimate and copy the overall industry's portfolio allocation. However, it is almost impossible to figure out the actual exposures and picking up a shift in the funds' exposures is only achievable with a certain delay. Another fundamental disadvantage is that with the purchase of such an ETF one acquires a basket that is too diverse to index – hedge funds are anything but a single asset class and therefore bundling them into an ETF leads to returns akin to those of a market index.[17]

- **Tracking holdings**: While imitating a widespread index does not seem to be sufficient, an alternative strategy for hedge fund ETFs is to analyse the holdings of the top performers by utilising the quarterly *Form 13F* filing investment managers have to report to the SEC to scan their favourite stocks and add them to the ETF's portfolio. But since the SEC grants fund managers a submission period of 45 days and the filings do not disclose short positions, the nature of the data is delayed and only provides half of the puzzle.[18]

- **Direct investment**: In principle, this seems the only reasonable strategy for hedge fund ETFs – but it is apparently limited to hedge funds with a managed account on the issuer's platform. Nonetheless, within the limited range of funds, this is an undistorted way to gain access to hedge fund exposure, even as a retail investor.[19]

Despite all of this, the attempt to provide accessibility for retail investors and liquidity to an illiquid asset comes at a price. On the one hand, the investor may face distortions as explained above and on the other hand, the ETF naturally charges fees exceeding the single hedge fund fees. Though beyond accessibility it may improve liquidity, the transparency issue remains unsolved or even enlarges due to the involvement of another intermediary.

On social trading platforms, any customer who fulfils the conditions to open a retail trading account can automatically replicate signals of traders on social trading platforms. Once registered and having funded the account, just a few clicks are necessary to compose a portfolio of traders and start copying their signals. As a consequence, social trading offers investors a higher level of accessibility that is not limited to the initial investment. Followers are empowered to autonomously control and actively intervene in their investments. The following list provides a brief overview of the most important features of accessibility and autonomy social trading platforms provide:

- **Manually intervene on positions**: As outlined earlier, followers can request an entire transaction history and manually intervene on replicated trader positions. Manual intervention means either closing the position or changing attributes like linked stop or limit orders. This is possible because the trades are replicated to their proprietary accounts and not executed within an external fund as with hedge or mutual funds.

- **Personalise replication settings**: Followers have the ability to set up the risk ratio with which they want to follow their chosen traders, down to the market level. By default, it is set to "1x". In this case, replication is proportional between trader and follower (based on the equity of their accounts). When adjusting this ratio, ayondo offers a fractional mapping of contract sizes to allow for exact proportionality. This way, the trader's performance can be replicated without distortion. A follower can even choose to completely exclude certain assets from being replicated to their account.

- **Stop/pause execution and automatic loss protection**: If a follower wants to close all positions replicated from traders in their portfolio and does not want to copy any further trades, the execution of their portfolio can be stopped or paused by a single click. It is even possible to automate this with a portfolio stop loss, to be triggered in case the equity reaches a predefined lower threshold.

- **Mobile accessibility**: Managing a portfolio of selected traders is not limited to desktop computers but can also be accomplished with a smartphone or tablet PC.

GOVERNANCE AND FRAUD

Within the last few years, hedge funds had been repeatedly subjected to fraud. The cause seems not to be hedge funds themselves, but the minimally regulated framework facilitating fraudulent activities. The variety of cases ranges from Ponzi schemes and insider trading to hiding suffered trading losses by manipulation of reports.[20] As a consequence, conflicts of interest may arise for a variety of reasons, e.g. side letters which may privilege certain investors to the disadvantage of others, multiple fund trades which may facilitate cross-subsidisation, and many other factors.[21] Especially in the US, some hedge funds do not use third parties as administrators or custodians of their assets, which may provoke conflicts of interest and can lead to fraud.

Since hedge funds have attracted the attention of the general public in recent years, a debated proposal is the introduction of a code of conduct. The UK brought such a code into force as a *comply or explain* approach, comparable to the German corporate governance code. In order to avoid being too restrictive, the rules are not obligatory, but the non-compliance of each paragraph has to be explained in a report which is published on a periodic basis. Altogether, this is expected to increase transparency and improve risk management – and finally to create disincentives to fraud.

On social trading platforms, users have to accept the *rules of the game* during their sign-up process, which is why signal providers on social trading platforms implicitly follow a mandatory code of conduct. Publishing trading signals only results in remuneration for a trader if they have accumulated followers – which is only possible by establishing a solid track record.

Since those track records are standardised and generated in real-time on an automated basis with the whole public as the audience, the possibility of fraud is very limited and would easily be exposed. Furthermore, in contrast to hedge funds, disincentives provided to the traders by side letter-like agreements with certain followers or cross-subsidisations between different accounts do not exist. The traders are unable to privilege certain followers by concluding individual agreements and therefore do not have an incentive to do so. Everyone receives the same trading signals for the same fees and therefore obtains the same return.

INNOVATION

Contrary to hedge funds, all social trading platforms are based on modern web technologies. In fact, most social trading companies are highly specialised software engineering firms rather than financial companies. This creates the basis for fast-paced innovation in social trading. Modern software engineering methods allow for short release cycles and rapid prototyping of new and innovative features. As described earlier, innovative compensation schemes like the ayondo career system can be realised quickly and effortlessly. Another example is the addition of real money traders, entering trading signals from real money broker accounts.

The traditional argument is that if a trader is using a virtual money account and not making a stake with their own capital, they may be tempted to gamble as it is impossible to suffer any real losses. However, humans tend to be averse to loss and behave more sensibly with regard to risk when assets are in the profit zone, and are more prone to risk once they are in a loss zone. This behaviour leads to the so-called *disposition effect* – traders hold on to losses for too long and realise profits too early.[22] Since he or she is not staking their own capital, this anomaly may be limited if a trader is trading with a virtual money account. The solution is to offer both real and virtual money accounts. Both can compete against each other and the followers can autonomously decide which framework provides better incentives.

CONCLUSION

Although *social trading* is a relatively new trend in financial markets, it provides investors access to an investment opportunity comparable to hedge funds but in contrast offering a higher level of transparency, liquidity and accessibility. This is achieved by using cutting-edge web technologies and modern software development methodologies to foster and speed up innovation cycles.

Furthermore, social trading platforms attract a wealth of traders who outperform the market on a risk-adjusted basis. Continuous advancement of technology and user functionality benefits investors by exposing them to various opportunities in order to gain access to alpha. One thing is certain: we currently are standing only at the very beginning of next generation hedge funds.

ENDNOTES

[1] HFR, report per Q2 2012.

[2] S. Paul, et al. (2013)

[3] W. Morris (1982).

[4] 'History of the Firm', A.W. Jones Advisers LLC, www.awjones.com/historyofthefirm.html.

[5] G. Connor and T. Lasarte (2011).

[6] Powell (2010).

[7] Directive 011/61/EU, see also dip21.bundestag.de/dip21/btd/17/122/1712294.pdf.

[8] Powell (2010).

[9] S. Paul et al., (2013).

[10] Carrie Johnson (2006).

[11] G. Cassar and J. Gerakos (2009).

[12] B. Liang (2000).

[13] R. Stulz (2010).

[14] AIFM-Umsetzungsgesetz (AIFM-UmsG).

[15] Directive 2011/61/EU.

[16] See e.g. Christopher Holmes (2009).

[17] Peter Davy (2012).

[18] Lewis Braham (2013).

[19] Peter Davy (2012).

[20] Federal Bureau of Investigation: Hedge Fund Information for Investors, see www.fbi.gov/about-us/investigate/white_collar/hedge-fund-fraud.

[21] Chris Day (2013).

[22] See D. Kahneman and A. Tversky, *Prospect Theory* (1979).

THE FUTURE OF FINANCE IS SOCIAL

BY ALON LEVITAN

ABOUT THE AUTHOR

Alon Levitan is Head of Strategic Marketing at eToro.

DISRUPTED BY THE INTERNET

IF THERE IS one driving force behind the changes to the financial services sector it is without any doubt the maturity of the internet and its users. The internet is the all-connecting superstructure offering a clean slate for every company and person to reinvent the ways people buy products and services, communicate with each other, educate themselves, socialise with their circles and inform themselves.

The innovations driven by faster open source development, faster go-to-market capabilities and the ability to test, learn and improve on the go have given many small, agile and focused companies the chance to disrupt established industries. Added to this is the mobile trend, which gives smartphone equipped users full access to all their online needs wherever they are.

For many people having access to the internet is equal to hitting the light switch – you just expect it to work, every time. A large number of people and businesses rely on the fact that they will always be on the internet in order to make a living. The number of internet-centric businesses is growing daily and so is the number of companies who integrate the internet into their business operations to generate alternative revenue streams.

Industries often fail to understand the far-reaching implications the internet will have on their business. Most often they move too slow for the inevitable progress fuelled by a better informed internet user, with instant access to other people to exchange and share information on anything of interest. Many large companies find it a challenge to adapt quick enough to the new business environment and will struggle to keep their dominance.

The internet has disrupted the publishing, music, entertainment, travel and hospitality industries. Many companies are still trying to figure out what the winning recipe is for integrating the *need for transparency* of the internet with their existing business practices. For many companies and industries full transparency can be harmful.

CHANGE IN THE FINANCIAL INDUSTRY

The financial industry is one of the few remaining strongholds that has managed to fend off the true power of the internet – let's call it *interconnected transparency* – and protect its shores from the flood. Certainly they have made small changes, for example many established companies like banks have expanded into online branches to service their customers online, but using the internet in this way is just an extension of the bank's traditional business at a much lower cost structure. That's good for business, especially since online banking services didn't require a fully transparent business practice at the time these services were introduced. Banks could still act like banks.

In a world where information is key to success, financial institutions always had the upper hand compared to the common people. The entire financial system is built to get hold of the information they need, process it faster than anyone else and make a profit executing on the information before someone else can. Let's call this *information arbitrage* – it is a quick, easy and sure way to generate profits.

What could not have been predicted in the early days of the internet was the emergence of the social phenomena. If the internet is the superstructure that physically connects every user and business then social is the layer on top of that superstructure that provides the personal connection. It's the personal connection that has propelled the internet into a different era; the era of full transparency. The internet has suddenly become more meaningful and the word *connection* is no longer a mere technical expression.

Apparently it was initially easier for people to expose their entire lives publically than for finance firms to get used to the idea of exposing their business practices. However, the internet has now started to disrupt and democratise the financial industry. Thomas Friedman's words "the world is flat" now also apply to the financial industry. I foresee the era of the walled garden banking system coming to an end, replaced with a more transparent financial system and more financially knowledgeable people.

Companies are being forced to play by the social rules because if they don't they could find themselves exposed on the social channel with a strong negative effect on their brand equity. No company, small or big, can afford to disregard the conversations between people on social networks about their brand, products and services without being actively engaged on these networks to protect themselves. Their brand is their most valuable asset and they cannot ignore this.

Major retail and investment banks have reached stellar heights in brand recognition and as such manage to retain their customers through their strong brand equity. These companies have poured billions of dollars into marketing and advertising to create the sense of security people need to entrust someone else with their money. However, once the money enters the financial system it is invisible to the people who put it there. They trust, often blindly, that these financial institutions know best what to do with their money. In their minds these are all money experts that know how to turn a profit.

In recent years even the strongest among the financial brands had to admit defeat, which has left deep cracks in the once impenetrable shield of trust. People started to question the untouchable reputation of these financial institutions. The big challenge today for many financial companies is how to embrace the need for more transparency without revealing their weaknesses. People are fed up with the current banking system, especially after several financial disasters caused by the irresponsible and overpaid members of the system. The expression "It's like money in the bank" is today to many consumers a much weaker promise than it used to be.

What if there was a different financial model that empowered people to take direct control over their financial assets, where the actual financial performance accounted for more than a brand promise and where information was shared openly?

THE EMERGENCE OF SOCIAL TRADING

The birth of social media has taught us all that people like to communicate and *a lot*. People are social animals and like to be part of a larger community. It provides a sense of belonging and protection.

Social media has given people the means to find other people of interest, like-minded individuals and long forgotten friends. Different social networks cater to different personal needs and provide a specialised social experience. As long as the focus of this network is on a subject of substantial interest, such as friends, jobs and money, then these networks will be able to attract and grow their user bases.

In the past two years the emergence of social investing and social trading as a specialised social network has received the people's stamp of approval as more and more users flock to create an interconnected investment community.

Gone are the walls that kept information secretive and exclusive to a few. Every piece of valuable information is shared openly and is able to be accessed by every member in these networks. Gone are the cover ups for bad investment decisions as trading performance and investment strategies are exposed openly. Gone is the black box era of banking and investing, with a new era of transparent investing where every person becomes accountable for their actions being ushered in.

Gone are the times of disconnected investors with no access to the people behind the financial brand. Now traders and money managers have to justify their investment strategies and actions to a more educated and better informed investor that is continuously monitoring their performance. Gone are the times where financial knowledge was confined to a selective few. In today's socially connected investment community people are sharing their knowledge freely and enjoy a reciprocal exchange of information to form better investment decisions.

Gone are the days where investing and trading was a lonesome activity. People come together to form tribes within networks, to connect on a personal level and provide each other with the moral support structure to overcome challenging investment periods.

WELCOME TO THE DEMOCRATISATION OF INVESTING

A social investment network embraces every member that is willing to share and contribute to the greater good of the community. This empowers every user in the network to become a tribe leader based on his or her trading performance and level of social interaction. By openly displaying their trading performance, investment strategy, portfolio breakdown and entire trading history, every user in the network conforms to the same principles of transparency to form a self-regulated investment community.

People are now able to find other traders based on their performance statistics, experience in specific markets and level of engagement within the community. People can consult with others on investment ideas and performance levels of other traders before making an investment decision. This level of access to information and to the actual people investing on behalf of the user will become standard in the financial industry and breakdown the black boxes where people deposit their funds and from that point on have no interaction with the people behind the trading strategy and execution.

Furthermore, the level of accountability for the executing trader has increased. Gone are the days where the investor doesn't know who the person or people investing their hard earned money are. In addition, a true social network with a mutually beneficial investment set up will require each member of the community to invest their own funds before they can be copied (*copying* is the eToro term for making the same trades as other users you are following) by other users in the network. This ensures equality among all invested parties and any investment risk applied by the trader is equally shared with all copying parties, and so are the potential returns of course.

eToro applies this important principle in its investment network. Research among our top performing traders confirms that they are investing more responsibly and averting risk where possible, especially if they have a large number of people copying their trades. Many of these tribe leaders acknowledge that it has transformed them into better traders as they are now taking responsibility for people's money they invest indirectly through the copy trading mechanism. This makes copy trading the fairest way to invest – knowing that the trader shares the same interest as the invested party.

For most traditional fund managers there is no necessity to invest their own money in the funds they manage, which disconnects the fund manager from the social responsibility to apply a more cautious investment approach with lower risk. Let's face it; if their own money isn't on the line then it's easier to take unnecessary risks to increase ROI performance. In the highly competitive investment fund market, each firm needs to shine through its performance to attract additional investors. The more investors, the more management fees the companies can charge their clients. However, these companies also charge client fees in the case of negative performance. Under this system the investor didn't only lose part of their invested capital, but also had to pay management fees for the generated loss.

This model is about to change and will reshape the investment arena. Pay on performance is going to be the new model users will seek. Social networks like eToro have long recognised this flaw in the current investment landscape and have shifted to a model where users are not paying any management fees for using the knowledge of other traders to invest their funds. We foresee no user opposition to the replacement of the current model of management fees with a system of paying out bonus fees to traders that have generated profits for their tribe members.

DIVERSIFICATION IS EVERYTHING

We already touched on the subject of copy trading and the way it is changing the investment landscape. With over 3m members eToro gives users access to a mature network with an active user base that is constantly sharing information about the markets with the entire community. This can either be in form of trending discussions or through actual executed trades, which provide insights into community sentiment for each of the available investment instruments.

Users have the great advantage of tapping into the wisdom of the crowd and making use of the collective knowledge of the network to benefit from emerging market trends. One of the more important indicators users are going to rely on is the number of copiers a trader/investor has attracted. This number creates a new data set to fuel what we refer to as *social analysis*. It complements traditional fundamental and technical analysis and provides an indicator that is more easy to comprehend for the mass market. The more copiers a user has attracted the better their performance will be. Social trading, driven by the copy trading technology, has also changed the way people apply risk diversification without the need to research every position in the investment portfolio.

We have all seen the TV show *Who wants to be a Millionaire?* and have witnessed the high rate of correct responses when the question is routed to the audience. This is also very true for investing and our analysis confirms that copy trading is up to 30% more profitable than manual trading.

With the simple click of a button, users can add or remove traders from their people-based portfolio. It boils down to choosing the right people to trade for you and the traded instruments become secondary. When copying several traders the user inherently adopts all investment strategies of all the copied users and this results in a highly diversified investment portfolio. Compare this to opening several accounts at banks and brokers to achieve the same – with high initial investment requirements to open accounts and other barriers this is an impossible task for most people.

Even if possible, how easy is it to shut down a broker or bank account and open a different one? In a social network switching funds between users is a matter of two clicks. No penalty fees, no switching fees and no other type of change-related fee.

PROTECTING THE USER

One of the challenges in dealing with the mass market is to ensure that every user joining the investment network is made aware of the risks involved when investing in the financial markets. The lack of knowledge is the main concern for why the majority of people are shying away from taking more ownership over their finances. Social trading enables every person to access the financial markets and to start investing in an easy, fun and engaging way.

As such it is imperative to educate the user and to implement protective measures until the user has reached *financial maturity*. Default settings need to protect users from unnecessary risk exposure, insufficient portfolio diversification and emotional investment decisions, which are the main reasons for loss of capital. eToro covers all of this through its built-in responsible trading features.

WHERE'S THE FUTURE OF FINANCE HEADING?

The financial world is already undergoing a change and this transformation will accelerate in the coming years, fuelled by the growing distrust of the operators in the current financial system. People will request high levels of transparency from their financial service providers and full accountability for investment decisions. Payouts to financial service providers will be based on performance only and investors will want to ensure investment goals are aligned between the end user and the financial institution.

Financial firms will have to compete with individual talent that can now expose their performance and attract people with an alternative investment opportunity. As more people become more knowledgeable about the financial markets they will start to take greater ownership of their finances and manage a larger portion of their funds directly or through the means of social trading (copy trading).

Large financial institutions will have to adapt to the more educated end user and will have to change their current investment products to be aligned with the new rules dictated by the empowered user. The internet and its social layer will be the driving force in the disruption of traditional finance and will force companies to reinvent themselves just like the publishing and music industries had to.

CROWDFUNDING: A FUNDAMENTAL CHANGE IN INVESTING

BY ZACK MILLER

ABOUT THE AUTHOR

Zack Miller is Partner, Head of Investor Community at OurCrowd, a leading online venture capital firm. Zack has been helping financial businesses grow for the past ten years by combining a deep knowledge of the finance/investment space with impactful, hands-on experience with internet businesses. He has held senior business positions or consulted to leading Finance 2.0 companies like Lending Club, Seeking Alpha, SigFig, Covestor, and Wall Street Survivor. He is the author of *Tradestream your Way to Profits: Building a Killer Portfolio in the Age of Social Media* (Wiley, 2010) and runs the successful blogs, Tradestreaming.com and NewRulesofInvesting.com. Zack holds an MBA from the Kellogg School of Management and a BA from Harvard University.

INTRODUCTION

FUNDAMENTAL SHIFTS HAPPEN in finance over long periods of time. The industry's slow adoption of consumer trends comes from a generally protective approach to regulation, making it harder to adopt trends exhibited in other consumer industries. But crowdfunding, the next logical step of a sweeping, multi-decade structural shift to do-it-yourself investing, threatens to disrupt all that. Though still in its early days, crowdfunding appears to be one of the few emerging trends that promises to fundamentally change the way we invest. The market is ripe for growth.

Crowdfunding draws its inspiration from a confluence of micro-finance and crowdsourcing.[1] Donation-based/rewards-based crowdfunding, long sidestepping securities laws because fundings are made as donations, not investments, was made popular by Kickstarter and Indiegogo. This success of these sites, raising over $1 billion for tens of thousands of projects, proves the model that entrepreneurs, artists and charities could turn to the internet to fund their projects. Lending Club, which has issued over $2.5 billion in person-to-person (p2p) loans, recently received an investment from Google at a reported $1.6 billion valuation.

Including all forms of crowdfunding, Deloitte Consulting expects the global industry to hit $5 billion this year and to grow at a CAGR of 100% over the near term. Equity crowdfunding is the next – and possibly the largest – leg in this trend.

CROWDFUNDING, OFFSHOOT OF CROWDSOURCING

To understand crowdfunding – investing in private companies by aggregating a large number of small investments from individuals (the *crowd*) – it's important to see it as part of a larger trend towards crowdsourcing. With crowdsourcing – tapping the collective intelligence, interest and activity of smart crowds of people over the internet – innovative companies are solving scientific problems, developing successful new products and improving the nature of teaching in the US K-12 school system. Crowdsourcing uses the internet to take the pulse of specific affinity communities, like educators, scientists and now investors, to solve problems, effect change and make a difference.

Crowdsourcing couldn't happen if people weren't participating in social networks, spending hours online every day. Media has moved from broadcast mode to one of participation, where readers not only consume content but create it. We're now a community of creators, with skin in the game when it comes to building and growing new, impactful things. Social media and crowdsourcing are two sides of the same coin.

Today's investors want in on this trend, too. According to a recent survey, over 30% of investors turn to social media for investing insights.[2] With 2012's huge Facebook IPO and headline-producing profiting of its early-stage investors, start-up investing is exciting compared to today's stock market. People want to invest in something big and exciting.

Part of this process means they also want to rally their friends and families to get involved in the same projects they're looking at. Crowdfunding answers this demand by making investing social and collaborative. Crowdfunding combines technology, social media and investing, representing what the future of investing might look like.

WHY FINANCE LAGS OTHER INDUSTRIES AND HOW IT'S CATCHING UP

While other industries are being completely disrupted by technology, finance finds itself in a funny position. As a user of technology (particularly, in research and trading), the financial field is among the most advanced sectors in the world. High Frequency Trading, for example, is entirely built upon exploiting momentary arbitrage opportunities via super powerful computer processing and extremely fast telecommunications connectivity.

But when it comes to the internet and empowering investors with new business models and frameworks, finance lags other industries. For example, in the area of travel and lodging, price comparison engines (like Kayak), peer-to-peer lodging (Airbnb) and new pricing models (Priceline.com) have permanently changed the way we plan, pay and experience travel. When it comes to investing, however, outside of being able to transact quicker and cheaper, we're still doing things the way we did 40 years ago.

Sure, we've got new start-up entrants in the investment management field attempting to attract new clients and users. Companies like Betterment, Wealthfront, and Personal Capital have attracted big interest from venture capitalists for their slick, web-based platforms that dispense automated, personalised investment advice. Covestor provides retail investors with unprecedented access to a marketplace of emerging investment managers. When it comes to changing the way we invest, though, these platforms are much more evolutionary than revolutionary.

So, why is finance so slow to ramp to internet speed? The US regulatory environment doesn't promote innovation as it protects investors by entrenching the status quo. New social media guidelines – a framework for financial professionals to take their businesses to where their clients spend time, on the internet – were introduced by the SEC and FINRA a couple of years back but they were ambiguous enough that the risk in adopting them still outweighs the reward for early adoption.[3]

Others might say that the present time is not right for innovation. In the wake of the 2009 recession, compliance requirements have become even stricter. In an environment like this, it would be disastrous for individuals to share – even accidentally – confidential and sensitive information. Instead of focusing on the enabling aspects of new technologies, most advancements in the financial/social media space cluster around archival and security applications, a necessary precursor towards any real embrace of social media.

ENTER CROWDFUNDING: IT BEGINS WITH A CHANGE IN REGULATION

Crowdfunding has been ushered in with a significant refocus of traditional securities laws, especially as they pertain to general solicitation and advertising. Due to their risky nature, private deals were traditionally relegated to sophisticated – *accredited*, according to the language of the SEC – investors. Early entrants to the equity crowdfunding space, like my firm OurCrowd, have done so in full-compliance with existing law by restricting their marketing and investment activity to accredited investors.

Here's a short history of recent regulatory moves in regards to crowdfunding:

1. **8 March 2012**: Congress signed the Jumpstart Our Business Startups Act (or, JOBS Act) to stimulate the creation of new jobs and to do so, Congress suggested encouraging investment in private companies (the primary engine of new job creation in the US).

2. **March 2013**: After passing Congress, the JOBS Act of 2012 was handed down to the SEC to determine exactly how the new rules should be implemented. In March of 2013, the SEC granted two "no-action" letters, the closest thing the regulatory body has to a blessing, officially clearing the way for equity crowdfunding for accredited investors only.

3. **23 September 2013**: This marked the first tangible change since the JOBS Act passed, paving the way to crowdfunding. After this date, private investments were allowed to be marketed publicly, reaching a much broader audience than was previously allowed by securities law. Investors will begin to see angel and venture capital deals popping up in their Facebook feeds and on Twitter. With the new rules for general solicitation and advertising in place, Silicon Valley's Route 101 is likely to be plastered with billboards touting the latest and greatest investment opportunities in private companies.

The next leg of the JOBS Act – and one that investors are still awaiting guidance on from the SEC – is the possibility to permit retail investors (non-*accredited*, non-*sophisticated* investors) to participate in private deals. This obviously opens up crowdfunding to a much larger audience and could make crowdfunding as ubiquitous as tax-deferred retirement plans.

Regardless of when the full gravitas of the JOBS Act will be felt, for the moment there are firms, like my firm OurCrowd, that have turned the internet into a platform for investing in private companies by limiting service to accredited investors.

THREE (AND GROWING) FLAVOURS OF CROWDFUNDING

At present there are three main flavours of crowdfunding:

1. Donations-based.
2. p2p.
3. Equity.

1. DONATIONS-BASED/REWARD-BASED CROWDFUNDING

As the regulatory environment becomes more supportive of crowdfunding, the crowdfunding industry is undergoing rapid growth. Crowdfunding's early successes have come from firms like Kickstarter and Indiegogo, which represent one form of crowdfunding: donation-based crowdfunding.

This form of crowdfunding involves project creators posting their financial needs to the internet in order to raise money to fund artistic pursuits (like a documentary movie) and social causes (like the adoption of stray animals). In return for their donations, individuals typically receive some type of commemorative object to mark their participation (for this reason, this form of fundraising is also called *rewards-based crowdfunding*).

To provide some context, in 2012 Kickstarter, the largest crowdfunding platform, raised $312m from over 2m backers, funding 18,000 projects. Even large companies are turning to these platforms to co-opt current and future customers into the product development cycle and get their feedback.

2. P2P LOANS

Another early entrant to crowdfunding is Lending Club, a marketplace for personal loans and a pioneer in the p2p lending arena. The site pairs individuals looking for small loans (on average, $12,000) and people willing to lend money in increments as small as $25. In return for taking on default risk, lenders receive interest payments that scale according to the creditworthiness of the borrower.

While the stock market has undulated over the past five years and we've seen some of the largest bankruptcies in US history, Lending Club investors are sitting pretty, having earned over $200m in interest payments over the same period. The site has facilitated more than $2.5 billion in loans since it was founded in 2007, as people grow more comfortable with borrowing outside of traditional banking channels for things like credit card consolidation and home-improvement.[4]

3. EQUITY CROWDFUNDING

In contrast, equity-based crowdfunding doesn't work via donations or rewards and it doesn't make loans. Instead, investors actually purchase equity in private companies in increments as small as $1000. Today, equity crowdfunding platforms, like OurCrowd, comply with security laws by restricting membership to accredited investors or high net-worth individuals.

Even if crowdfunding doesn't make its way to the retail investor, high net worth (HNW) investors are already using these types of platforms to fund private equity. According to the Royal Bank of Canada (RBC), there is over $45 trillion of capital in high net worth (HNW) individuals' hands worldwide. In the US, Carlyle estimates there is $10 trillion in over 5m US accredited households, justifying the private equity firm's own surprising announcement to reduce the minimum investment in their private equity funds from $20m to only $50,000.

This money is looking for a home: according to April's Northern Trust survey of HNW investors, more than half of HNW investors are actively seeking new investments to increase their wealth, while 30% are more inclined to consider alternative investments than they were five years ago.

GROWTH OF THE MARKET

According to a recent survey from Crowdsourcing.org,[5] $1.5 billion was allocated to crowdfunding platforms worldwide in 2011 and 2012 nearly doubled that, reaching almost $3 billion.

Across the three categories outlined above, the market currently breaks down to:

1. **Donation and rewards-based crowdfunding**: grew 85% to $1.4 billion.
2. **Consumer lending** (peer-to-peer): grew 111% to $1.2 billion.
3. **Equity crowdfunding**: grew 30% to $116m.

Regional growth

Crowdfunding is a global phenomenon but North America and Europe are leading the way, raising much more money via crowdfunding than the rest of the world. Here's how the global crowdfunding market breaks down by geography:

1. **North America**: topped $1.6 billion in 2012, growing 105%.
2. **Europe**: grew 65% to $945m.
3. **Rest of World (ROW)**: grew 125%, to almost $200m.

The world is watching closely the US implementation of the JOBS Act. The JOBS Act, either in its current limited form or in its full regalia, represents some very forward-thinking liberalisation of securities laws. It places the US at the forefront of the path to crowdfunding.

HOW DEALS GET DONE: THE SOCIAL DYNAMICS OF CROWDFUNDING

Crowdfunding projects are in large part impacted by the social networks of the project's founders (much like friends and family sources in the offline world). To take an average project in the film category, a founder with ten Facebook friends would have a 9% chance of succeeding, one with 100 friends would have a 20% chance of success and one with 1000 friends would have a 40% chance of success.[6]

The social nature of crowdfunding campaigns typically means that 25% to 40% of the revenue raised comes from first to third degree connections of the project owners.[7] While the future for crowdfunding is truly global – imagine an American investor being able to make private investments in startups all over the world – the strong social nature of crowdfunding projects does contribute to some of the same home-bias in crowdfunding that we see in the stock market.[8]

CURATED VS. OPEN PLATFORMS

Crowdfunding platforms – especially those focused on equity crowdfunding – are faced with an important decision in servicing their investors: do they entirely embrace the marketplace ethos and create a fully-open platform that any start-up can raise money on, or do they take a more walled-garden approach, doing much of the initial due diligence to help ensure investors get access to high-quality opportunities?

AngelList has taken the same approach as Google's Android and created an open platform for any start-up around the world to announce that it is raising money. OurCrowd, on the other end of the spectrum, is following the Apple iOS gameplan, requiring strict compliance to due-diligence criteria in order to take investments from the crowd, weeding out the majority of opportunities that don't make the cut. Both approaches have merit and both appeal to different types of investors.

FUTURE OF CROWDFUNDING: COMING TO A THEATRE NEAR YOU

The advent of crowdfunding platforms threatens to change the transactional model the finance industry has in place (stock markets, broker-dealers, market makers, clearing firms, etc.). Instead of turning to a broker or advisor to make an investment on the stock market, crowdfunding encourages direct investments into smaller firms. Many of these firms don't charge management fees, choosing instead to share in the potential upside of profits.

As crowdfunding grows, expect to see secondary markets created by the crowdfunding platforms themselves, injecting much-needed liquidity into a generally illiquid asset class. NASDAQ, the US's second largest stock market, may already see the writing on the wall. In March 2013, the stock exchange announced[9] a partnership with SharesPost, one of the leading marketplaces of private company shares. In an environment where many firms would prefer to remain private, the NASDAQ Private Market could be the remaking of the modern stock market but for private shares.

Crowdfunding is also seriously changing the way people identify investments. Younger investors may prove to be more hands-on than the generation that stored their wealth in mutual funds held in their tax-deferred retirement plans. Crowdfunding appeals to investors who like to roll up their sleeves, research their own opportunities and invest in projects, ideas, and entrepreneurs who are building tomorrow's successful enterprises. Layer in the social element, with investors building online reputations, followers and influence, and the entire investing process begins to look more like how the internet has transformed other industries.

Some of the winners in the crowdfunding space will be broad marketplaces where investors can find opportunities in multiple industries. But, there's an arms race underway to develop industry-specific environments, where investors interested in a particular niche can drill-down to find the most interesting opportunities. Think doctors investing in medical device companies and teachers in educational start-ups. Investors will soon have the opportunity to deploy capital in horizontal and vertical crowdfunding sites.

Beyond the industry-specific, crowdfunding – especially in equity crowdfunding, which competes relatively directly with traditional venture capitalists – might spell the death of geography[10] for a private equity process currently dominated by local players with boots on the ground. Though early crowdfunding investors are still likely to invest in local opportunities even online, the global nature of the web will mean a more efficient allocation of investment capital towards deserving opportunities.

Crowdfunding, in its numerous forms, is the perfect storm needed to disrupt finance. By combining micro-finance with crowdsourcing, this form of investing has already begun to attract tens of thousands of investors from around the world who value the autonomy, the diversity of opportunities and the social nature of crowdfunding. In an industry that is generally sceptical of harbingers of change, far-sighted finance professionals are already placing their bets on the future of finance... and that's crowdfunding.

ENDNOTES

[1] www.forbes.com/sites/tanyaprive/2012/11/27/what-is-crowdfunding-and-how-does-it-benefit-the-economy

[2] BMO InvestorLine Study, www.marketwired.com/press-release/repeat-bmo-investorline-study-despite-rise-social-media-investors-still-rely-on-traditional-tsx-bmo-1824137.htm

[3] econsultancy.com/il/blog/62215-why-has-the-financial-services-sector-been-slow-to-adopt-social

[4] blog.lendingclub.com/2012/11/07/five-year-review-lending-club-notes-outpace-stocks-and-bonds

[5] '2013CF – The Crowdfunding Industry Report', masssolution.com, www.crowdsourcing.org/editorial/2013cf-the-crowdfunding-industry-report/25107

[6] Ethan R. Mollick, 'The Dynamics of Crowdfunding: An Exploratory Study', *Journal of Business Venturing* (26 June, 2013). Available at SSRN: ssrn.com/abstract=2088298 or dx.doi.org/10.2139/ssrn.2088298

[7] Mollick, 'The Dynamics of Crowdfunding'.

[8] Mingfeng Lin and Siva Viswanathan, 'Home Bias in Online Investments: An Empirical Study of an Online Crowd Funding Market' (16 February 2013). Available at SSRN: ssrn.com/abstract=2219546 or dx.doi.org/10.2139/ssrn.2219546

[9] venturebeat.com/2013/03/06/nasdaq-private-market

[10] Mollick, Ethan R., The Dynamics of Crowdfunding: An Exploratory Study (June 26, 2013). *Journal of Business Venturing*, 2013 (Forthcoming). Available at SSRN: ssrn.com/abstract=2088298 or dx.doi.org/10.2139/ssrn.2088298

3

NEW FINANCIAL BUSINESS MODELS THAT EMPOWER CONSUMERS

INTELLIGENT INDEX ENGINEERING: A NEW WAY OF PRESENTING ACTIVE ASSET ALLOCATION STRATEGIES

BY DR STEVEN J. BATES

ABOUT THE AUTHOR

Steven Bates is CEO of QLAB Invest Ltd., a specialist in systematic investment advisory and active index engineering. QLAB's philosophy is to embrace active asset selection and sound risk management principles in order to develop non-subjective investment strategies across asset classes globally. Steven has a Ph.D. in Physics from the University of Cambridge in the UK and CERN in Switzerland.

INTRODUCTION

INNATE HUMAN BEHAVIOUR and biases drive more of the financial market dynamics than one might expect.

Whilst not strongly predictable, the dynamics can nevertheless be exploited as they are also not completely random. Systematic investment strategies making use of directional signals as well as innovative risk management techniques can result in well-behaved investment portfolios which are less prone to the left-tail risk seen in most passive and many active strategies.

Each strategy is turned into an *intelligent index* allowing potential investors to monitor risk and performance separately and decide through what kind of vehicle they want to access the strategy.

Separating strategy from delivery empowers investors by allowing them to choose the investment method and regulatory framework that best suits their needs. It also allows providers to focus on their core competences and does not force them to try to master all parts of the value chain.

Finally, indexing an active strategy sets the highest possible level of integrity, transparency and efficiency, which is in the best interests of the investor.

1. BEHAVIOURAL MARKET DYNAMICS

What could possibly link an iceberg, Albert Einstein and financial markets?

Most people would say that 10% of an iceberg sits above water and 90% below and I shall use this concept as a model for the human brain. In this model the part that sits above water is your conscious self, the *you* that is with you all the time, your inner voice, a problem solver that can be educated and the you that makes important, rational decisions. So you think.

The part that sits below water is our subconscious, emotional self and the source of our gut feelings. Not just responsible for keeping us breathing and alive whilst sleeping, it has kept us alive over countless generations. When humans lived on plains, hunting, gathering and caring for our young, this part of our brain meant survival. It is the oldest and most powerful part of us. The model serves as a reminder that behind the *you* that you think you know best there lurks a much more powerful agent that works automatically and very fast.

We don't notice our subconscious working; it is effortless and almost instantaneous. But whilst it makes use of shortcuts or heuristics to quickly model the world around us (keeping us alive) it can also make mistakes. It can be fooled by the modern world in such a way that leads to biases and even prejudices which affect our actions and our decisions.

One of the leading authorities on the subject is the Nobel Prize winning psychologist Daniel Kahneman. His best-selling book *Thinking, Fast and Slow* is essential reading. It turns out that not only are we often not aware of these effects, but importantly we cannot control them. There is overwhelming evidence that financial market participants are not always acting rationally – quite the opposite in fact. It turns out that this irrationality drives a large part of financial market dynamics.

Now consider Einstein's famous equation $E=mc^2$, which states that energy, E and mass, m are related. They are two facets of the same property, linked through a fundamental constant of nature, the speed of light, c. As part of more complex chemical and biological process the energy-mass equivalence principle helps explain how energy comes from the sun, how a tree can turn sunlight into apples and how your body can turn food into a game of football. In all cases mass is turned into energy, or vice versa.

The equation is a reminder of how nature works through cause and effect. Hydrogen nuclei in the sun collide and fuse to create helium, releasing energy in the form of photons of light. Some of the hydrogen's mass is converted into photons according to Einstein's equation. Some photons travel to earth and are converted back into mass and may end up as apples. Some photons may hit your skin and cause cancer. Cause and effect at work. We know how a skin cell is damaged by the photon but we cannot predict when such events will happen exactly.

Luckily we can study such natural processes in enormous detail and understand a great deal. Even without being able to predict such things in advance the science of statistics allows us to understand many properties of nature. Two of the best books on the subject are *How Nature Works* by Per Bak and *Critical Mass* by Philip Ball.

Can this kind of scientific thinking help us understand financial markets? Consider the third image in the illustration above – a snapshot of the performance of the S&P 500. Are the dynamics of this market driven by cause and effect, i.e. deterministic, or are they random, or perhaps something in between? Behavioural finance research has found that despite what we think about being in control of our thoughts and actions, a more powerful agent inside all of us can lead us to react and behave in certain ways and this has an observable impact on financial market dynamics.

There is very strong evidence that markets do not follow Gaussian statistics (normal distribution), but rather a so-called power law which has much fatter tails than the normal distribution. This means that larger movements (typically to the downside) occur much more frequently than expected. There is also some evidence that markets behave similarly to so-called self-organised critical systems which are characterised by periods of relative calm punctuated by high activity.

One reason for this is that investors often act together en masse. The so-called momentum effect in markets is well documented, whereby investor herding creates persistence in movement. This movement is visible as steady trends (up or down), bubbles (irrational exuberance) and market crashes (fear or panic). This doesn't mean that the movements are necessarily predictable in advance but human behaviour genetically engrained in all of us cannot change easily or quickly and the observable market dynamics show persistent properties. This allows for exploitation. A wonderfully written book on the subject of applying statistical models to investing and avoiding behavioural mistakes is *The Naked Portfolio Manager* by Robert J. Fischer.

Scientific methods used to study how nature works can be applied to financial markets and show that the dynamics are driven to a large extent by the innate biases and reactions of the countless market participants. Research has shown that we can understand a great deal about the properties through statistics and also that the dynamics may be exploited.

However, any methods of exploiting these dynamics must be engineered in a way which does not suffer from the very biases causing them, i.e. they must be systematic and based on a solid quantitative foundation.

2. ACTIVE ASSET ALLOCATION

FOUR-ASSET MODEL

Let us first create a simplified model of the financial market. Suppose the market consists of four risky assets (US equities, commodities, US treasury bonds and currencies) plus a non-risky asset (cash). If an investor's liquid wealth is not sitting in physical paper money under the mattress (which it can and occasionally does), it is in electronic cash deposits or some risky but liquid security from the four asset class set.

From time-to-time the investor moves money between the various assets and cash. The relative amount of money moving between assets affects their prices. In a liquid, normally operating market if there are more buyers than sellers of a particular asset then its price increases and if the opposite occurs its price decreases.

In this highly simplified model we are essentially observing where the money or value is in the financial system by the relative movements in prices – this is analogous to the equation $E=mc^2$ where energy can neither be created nor destroyed. The interesting thing about this model is that a reason why there are more buyers than sellers causing prices to move is not needed. There is simply some cause which affects prices.

The science of statistics based on robust quantitative methods can be used to measure a whole host of properties of price movements. The most common measures are return and volatility (a measure of risk), but it's also important to look a little deeper. Correlation of returns between assets tells us how assets move together and analysing distributions of returns also reveals properties about the symmetry of gains and losses (skewness) as well as the tails of the distribution (excess kurtosis).

Whilst not everyone is familiar with these properties, we can learn a lot about the underlying movements in markets from relatively few measures. Interestingly, they are all derived essentially from just one input – price.

Now consider Figure 2, which shows the actual one-year rolling returns of the four asset classes in the model over the last 30 years. A strong bias to positive annual returns is immediately observable, which is evidence of a risk premium (return in excess of the risk free rate). Also, whenever one or more assets loses value for at least a year (as shown by the shaded areas), there is always one or more that are gaining in value. This is logical as investors move their money around the system searching for returns or relative safety.

Proponents of modern portfolio theory (MPT) or passive management would say hold all the assets and pick up the risk premium, the so-called free lunch, but as we shall see in a moment there is considerable risk with this approach.

Figure 2 – rolling one-year returns of US equities, Commodities (CCI), 5YR US Treasuries and G10 currencies long versus USD

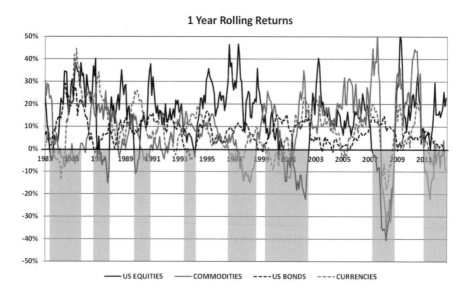

SIGNALS FROM STATISTICAL PROPERTIES OF GROUP INVESTING

There are many factors that can cause a particular individual to act independently or with the herd, to be greedy, fearful or to panic. But take all investors together and certain statistical properties appear. Like the grains in a sand pile, sometimes something triggers off a chain of events, cause and effect, which can have a sudden big impact. At other times things progress in certain directions over long periods of time rather steadily.

My research has shown that over the short to medium term (measured in days and weeks rather than months and years):

- Risk as measured by price volatility is rather predictable -> autocorrelation of risk.

- Trend (market direction) is somewhat predictable -> momentum effect.

- Risk and trend are linked -> greed and fear at work.

- Correlation between assets is highly variable and cannot be predicted -> market shocks.

- Price movements can be far greater than expected from conventional statistical models based on the Gaussian distribution -> panic causes fat left tails.

These properties can be exploited using quantitative methods to create signals that indicate which assets should be favoured at which time. There is no long-term prediction involved, just reaction to current conditions which tend to show persistence. Given conditions can change at any time the process of generating signals must be repeated often and it turns out that a monthly process works well.

More importantly, a human should not be involved in the signal generation in order not to fall foul of the behavioural traps. This means the signal generation should be systematic, i.e. determined by quantitative and statistical algorithms, and no discretionary interventions should take place.

Signals (buy, hold or sell) themselves do not constitute an investment strategy and a portfolio must be constructed from the signals which is a risk management task. Further, the risk management process must take into account certain truths about the markets:

1. Returns are not normally distributed and exhibit fat tails due to sudden sell-offs.

2. Diversification based on using historic correlations as favoured in MPT can fail over the short term. It is also important to build in certain hard constraints to limit exposures between, as well as within, asset classes. This is just part of sensible portfolio construction.

3. It should be emphasised that nobody has a crystal ball, any model has its weaknesses and markets remain in many ways fundamentally unpredictable.

In essence the signalling and risk management task is to use what information can be gleaned to improve performance and risk characteristics versus some alternative strategy. What are the possible alternative approaches? There is actually an interesting evolution occurring in the index world and it is worth spending some time on this.

INDEX METHODOLOGY EVOLUTION

Figure 3 – evolution of index methodologies

INDEX EVOLUTION	WEIGHTING METHOD	ACTIVITY
SINGLE ASSET MARKET	MARKET CAPITALISATION (EQUITIES), OUTSTANDING DEBT (BONDS)	PASSIVE
MULTI ASSET MARKET	BENCHMARK OR FIXED MIX	PERIODIC REBALANCING
SINGLE ASSET "SMART"	EQUAL WEIGHT, RISK WEIGHTED, MINIMUM VOLATILITY, FUNDAMENTAL …	PERIODIC REBALANCING
MULTI ASSET "SMART"	DYNAMIC ASSET ALLOCATION	ACTIVE
RISK OVERLAY (SINGLE OR MULTI ASSET)	DYNAMIC ASSET ALLOCATION	ACTIVE

Figure 3 shows how index construction is evolving. Most people are familiar with single asset market indices such as the S&P 500 which is perhaps the most used barometer of equity market performance. This is a market capital weighted index which means larger companies, i.e. companies that have performed well, have a larger weight in the index. Whilst it may be a simple and well established approach, there are two main issues with market capital weighted indices.

Firstly, a few large companies can come to dominate an index and diversification suffers. Secondly, investing in the index means buying the equities that increased most in price and selling those that decreased most which can be detrimental to performance due to mean reversion of prices which occurs from time to time. A similar thing occurs with bond aggregate indices which are usually weighted according to amount of debt outstanding. These passive indices are cheap to access as they do not require rebalancing, however this lack of activity can be a source of great risk for the investor.

Then there are multi-asset market indices which offer greater diversification across asset classes such as equities, bonds and commodities. The starting part or default allocation is a fixed mix of assets, essentially a benchmark. Periodic rebalancing brings assets back to their target weights. Benchmark investing is nothing new and asset managers and banks have been offering portfolio solutions based on benchmarks for many years, however the publication of multi-asset indices is relatively new.

So far there are only very few products tracking multi-asset benchmarks despite it arguably being a simple way of accessing the market beta or risk premium as evidenced in Figure 2. This may be due to the fact that so many passive single-asset building blocks exist already and a benchmark portfolio can be built up using a few single-asset products rather than one multi-asset product. Indeed there are many supporters of passive investing who state it is not possible to beat the market so therefore the best approach is to invest in a few low-cost tracking products, rebalance from time-to-time and relax.

A further innovation over recent years has been the rise of so-called *smart beta* indices on single assets. There are many variations but they include: equal weighting, risk weighting and fundamental weighting. An example is the S&P 500 Equally Weighted Index, launched in 2003, where each of the 500 stocks has an index weight of 0.2%. These methods have a degree of activity in that they are rebalanced from time-to-time which adds cost but supporters argue the higher diversification and greater return potential more than compensates.

It is worth noting that the simple activity of rebalancing forces the selling of securities which have increased in price and the buying of securities which have decreased in price. There is evidence that due to mean reversion of prices this rebalancing can already add value irrespective of the underlying asset weighting method.

I believe though that the index evolution should not stop there. Passive single-asset, market and smart beta indices are missing an active risk management element, which is the ability to underweight or even exit a risky asset when it declines. It is not much comfort if the S&P 500 declines 50%, the smart beta index declines 40% and the balanced market index declines 30%. Surely an investor would rather hold a different asset for a while, perhaps even cash.

Further, using the same systematic risk processes it is possible to create overlays which improve the characteristics of underlying passive indices. Whilst active asset allocation and risk overlays are traditionally a portfolio or risk management task I believe that building what is essentially a market timing approach into an index can offer significant value to investors and I will return to this in the final section.

ACTIVE STRATEGY VERSUS MULTI-ASSET MARKET INDEX

For the purpose of finding out how successful a truly active strategy is I have chosen to compare performance to a multi-asset market index. Using Figure 2 again, I define the reference portfolio as holding those four risky assets plus cash with fixed starting weights and rebalancing them from time to time.

The weights are: 25% US equities equally weighted across sectors, 25% commodities equally weighted (CCI), 20% G10 currencies long against USD equally weighted and

30% equally weighted in USD cash, 2YR treasury and 5YR treasury. I named this portfolio "Naive" given that it is simple but arguably inefficient from a risk management perspective.

Figure 4 shows the comparison of a quantitative active strategy[1] versus the naive portfolio as well as the S&P 500 calculated over the last 30 years. Note the active strategy has been live and unchanged since 1 July 2010, uses no shorting or leverage and is simply trying to navigate to the right assets at the right time.

Figure 4 – performance and risk of the active and naive strategies

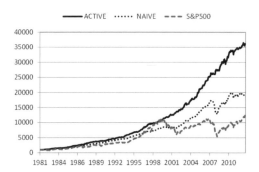

	ACTIVE	NAIVE	S&P500
ANNUAL RETURN	11.6%	9.5%	8.0%
VOLATILITY	5.4%	6.8%	15.3%
MAX DRAWDOWN	-5.3%	-25.8%	-52.6%
SKEW	0.07	-0.71	-0.66
E. KURTOSIS	1.50	4.16	2.25
SHARPE RATIO	1.14	0.58	0.16
CASH ANNUAL RETURN	5.5%		

The S&P 500 had the roughest ride over the last 13 years with two periods of dramatic sell-off (fear and some panic at work) which is a stark reminder that passively investing only in equities can require patience as well as strong nerves to get at the risk premium. With the naive portfolio the investor does indeed earn a reasonable risk premium of about 4% per year with a volatility of 7%.

However, the short-term volatility and drawdown risk can be much higher than expected and an unlucky investor who invested in March 2007 would have been sitting on a loss of over 25% a year later, a nasty surprise for someone expecting a free lunch. This investor would not have seen a profit until almost three years later, if indeed they had stayed invested. Studies have shown that following a sudden loss investors often pull out of the market in fear and thus never experience the recovery. This is hardly relaxing for the investor.

As stated before, the main problem with the S&P 500 and the naive market portfolio is the lack of active risk management. By comparison the active strategy has neutralised the left-tail risk and greatly improves risk-adjusted return, as seen by the following measures:

- Annual return is increased by more than 2% over the naive portfolio. This comparison was made fair by subtracting 0.3% per year from the active strategy to account for the increased cost of trading whilst the naive portfolio has no costs deducted (despite the fact that rebalancing would carry some cost).

- Average risk, or volatility, is lower and although not shown on this chart the risk measured over shorter time frames is more stable.

- Maximum drawdown (largest peak to trough loss) is just -5%, versus -26% for the market portfolio and -53% for the S&P 500, which doesn't just save the investor's capital but also it prevents them panicking and selling at the wrong time.

- Skewness of monthly returns, which is a measure of how much a return distribution is biased toward losses or gains, is transformed from negative (bad) to positive (good).

- Excess kurtosis of monthly returns, which is measure of the tail fatness, is greatly reduced.

- Risk adjusted return, as shown by the Sharpe ratio, is greatly improved.

Whilst these properties are a testament that active management can add value, another view shows something else. Figure 5 shows rolling one-year returns of the active strategy against the naive market portfolio over 30 years of simulation. The asymmetry of returns, known as convexity, is remarkable. It shows that when the market is declining, the active strategy is able to stay positive and make a modest return. When the market is increasing the active portfolio is able to keep up.

This dynamic beta property is what investors should really be interested in. Investors should not be concerned about beating the market continuously but specifically beating the market when it goes down and keeping up with the market when it goes up. Professional traders might recognise this kind of payoff as a *call option* which is also referred to as being *long volatility*. This is considered by many to be a healthy position to hold in general.

Figure 5 – rolling returns of the active versus the naive strategy

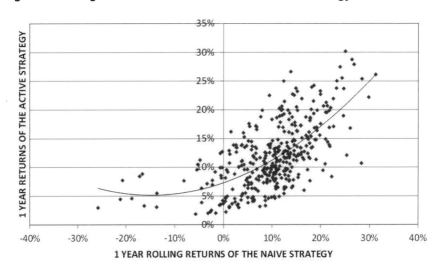

COMBINED PASSIVE INDEX AND CASH POSITION

Despite the potential to improve multi-asset investing in an active strategy I also recognise that some investors prefer to construct portfolios on a single asset basis. So is there a way to soften the roller coaster ride of holding on to the S&P 500 evident in Figure 4?

One answer is to use a risk overlay to mix the passive index with a cash position. Short-term risk and performance information is used to scale the exposure down from 100%, adding cash as risk increases or performance declines, and then scale exposure up again when conditions allow. Figure 6 shows this rather simple risk process can improve the properties of a passive index like the S&P 500, decreasing volatility and drawdown and transforming skew to the positive.

The improvement in annual return is a consequence of not having participated so much in the drawdowns. This kind of overlay strategy is not designed to outperform per se but rather to offer good upside capture with improved risk characteristics. The process works across regional or global equities and can also be used to create leveraged solutions scaling exposure beyond 100% should investors seek higher risk profiles.

Figure 6 – risk overlay model applied to the S&P 500

	S&P500	RISK OVERLAY
ANNUAL RETURN	8.0%	9.3%
VOLATILITY	15.3%	9.8%
MAX DRAWDOWN	-52.6%	-20.0%
SKEW	-0.66	0.09
E. KURTOSIS	2.25	1.35
SHARPE RATIO	0.16	0.38

3. CLIENT-CENTRIC SOLUTIONS

If done carefully, simulating or backtesting a strategy can provide evidence that an active strategy works in practice, however a few additional conditions and tests must be made before developing client solutions:

- A systematic strategy should not be calibrated or optimised based on historic data. This is sometimes referred to as *curve fitting*. It is easy, with perfect hindsight, to create a strategy which delivered superior returns. Instead the strategy must be non-calibrated and stable, i.e. not constantly changed, which by the way would render it discretionary rather than systematic and means it may fall foul of the most common behavioural traps.

- An active strategy should take into account liquidity and costs of trading. No strategy can be active if there is no liquidity and thus the choice of underlying assets must undergo analysis for liquidity, even in times of crises. Secondly there is a cost to trading (brokerage fees and bid-offer spreads mainly) and the strategy should be shown net of these costs to give a fair picture.

- The strategy should undergo stress testing under real as well as fictitious market conditions to understand a wide range of behaviour, for example what happens if interest rates rise, if there is an equity bear market or if markets crash?

- The strategy should not be a complete *black box*. Whilst the strategy may contain considerable intellectual property and it may not be possible to reveal all details publicly the designers should be as transparent as possible, especially to potential investors. They should be able to explain clearly how the strategy works and also where any potential weaknesses and risks might be.

- The strategy should be monitored live for a while with its algorithms unchanged and money invested to establish live performance and risk statistics, which is a final test of potential curve fitting.

INTELLIGENT INDEX ENGINEERING

One way to meet these conditions is to turn the strategy into an investable index which is published independent of any solutions being managed. An index, if correctly constructed, represents an accurate calculation of the performance of the strategy net of replication costs. Creating an index requires a high level of diligence, integrity and transparency. Investment banks can confirm the feasibility and costs of investing as well as the potential replication methods available. Independently, small amounts of money can be run to confirm returns are achievable in practice.

I refer to this as *intelligent index engineering* and there are considerable benefits for the investor:

- Ensures the highest possible level of systematic discipline, liquidity and cost analysis.

- Improves transparency over comparable strategies available only as funds.

- Visible and auditable performance and risk track record independent of assets or products.

- Separation of strategy and investment access means investors have considerable flexibility in accessing the strategy.

It is this last point that allows for the development of truly client-centric solutions, empowering the investor. Why should a strategy provider that has excellent quantitative skills also be excellent in managing and distributing funds or in providing discretionary asset management services?

Undoubtedly some large banks or asset managers possess all the necessary skills, but the separation of strategy from delivery allows a strategy provider to focus on their core competences and does not force them to master all parts of the value chain. Let us also not forget the conflicts of interest linked to having all tasks under one roof, from tinkering with investment processes to manipulating fund NAVs to downright fraud (à la Madoff).

PRODUCTS AVAILABLE TO THE INVESTOR

There is considerable choice of product delivery available to the investor which depends on such factors as size of assets, domicile, preferred regulatory structure and also investment guidelines for institutions. In order of increasing asset size the main product formats are shown in Figure 7.

Figure 7 – the main product formats

PRODUCT FORMAT	SINGLE CLIENT / POOLED VEHICLE	TYPICAL LIQUIDITY	ASSETS REQUIRED TO LAUNCH
CONTRACT FOR DIFFERENCE (CFD) PLATFORM	SINGLE	CONTINUOUS	< 1,000 USD
BROKER MANAGED ACCOUNT	SINGLE	CONTINUOUS	
BANK MANAGED ACCOUNT	SINGLE	CONTINUOUS	1 – 5M USD
ACTIVELY MANAGED CERTIFICATE	SINGLE / POOLED	CONTINUOUS	
OFFSHORE FUND	SINGLE / POOLED	WEEKLY / MONTHLY	5 – 10M USD
ONSHORE FUND	POOLED	DAILY	25 – 50M USD
ETF	POOLED	CONTINUOUS	>50M USD

Contract for difference platforms such as ayondo (www.ayondo.com) and Gekko Global Markets (www.gekkomarkets.com) offer an interesting and relatively new option either to test strategies with modest amounts of money, or attract investors who do not typically invest in pooled vehicles or who do not have enough assets for other solutions.

Managed accounts offer great flexibility for investors with more assets and the option to customise strategies and set individual pricing. These features would generally not be available to smaller investors as they are not scalable for providers unless they have a strong technical infrastructure behind them (although such solutions are gradually becoming more commonplace).

Actively Managed Certificates represent an attractive option as they can be considered an *ETF-light* solution. Not being as tightly regulated as ETFs or other funds they are much cheaper and can be exchange traded providing continuous liquidity and end-of-day or NAV dealing. Also, issuer credit risk can be removed through collateralisation and asset segregation.

Finally, conventional fund solutions are also possible, however setup and running costs can be high (a drag on performance) unless large asset size is available. Increased regulation, whilst attempting to protect investors, has actually led to greatly increased costs which may be fine for the largest institutions but presents a challenge to newer and smaller providers.

4. SUMMARY

Intelligent index engineering is a new way of presenting active asset allocation and risk overlay strategies. This approach combines the benefits of active management (asset selection and risk management) with passive management (high liquidity, transparency and low fees). The index engineering process imposes a high level of integrity and is based on a combination of human psychology, quantitative methods and product innovation expertise.

In summary:

- Behavioural finance research shows considerable evidence that irrational choice making, greed and fear drive a large part of financial market dynamics.

- Statistical research shows that markets are not random nor are they strongly predictable, however they exhibit enough persistence to be exploited with systematic strategies.

- Truly systematic active asset allocation strategies can provide superior performance and lower risk than passive or benchmark investing.

- Strategies can be complete single or multi-asset portfolios or work as overlays on top of existing portfolio building blocks.

- A new level of integrity and transparency can be reached by publishing strategies as *intelligent* indices.

- Investors are thus able to monitor and analyse the strategy before investing and then choose a particular investment vehicle and replication method which suits them best.

BIBLIOGRAPHY

Bak, Per, *How Nature Works* (Copernicus, 1996)

Ball, Philip, *Critical Mass: How One Thing Leads To Another* (Arrow Books, 2005)

Fischer, Robert J., *The Naked Portfolio Manager* (Abalucci Press, 2009)

Kahneman, Daniel, *Thinking, Fast and Slow* (Allen Lane, Penguin Group, 2011)

ENDNOTE

[1] The active strategy is the Spectrum Absolute Return Index, www.qlabi.com/spectrum-idx.asp.

THE NETWORKED BANK

BY JOHN EGAN

ABOUT THE AUTHOR

John Egan is the CEO of Sandbox AG, the foremost global community of leaders and innovators under 30. Sandbox accelerates the world's most exceptional young leaders from the point of local impact to global influence. Sandbox's ambition is that every person on the planet will be positively effected by the work of a Sandboxer.

Additionally, John is an expert on the future of banking. He has a BComm in Finance from University College Dublin and a MSc in Finance and Econometrics. John has worked in finance in the US and Europe and has previously started and sold businesses in the engineering sector. He is a speaker and contributor to a number of books and publications including 'New Ideas, New Ireland' and his eBook on the future of retail banks has been downloaded over 180,000 times.

He is the founder and benefactor of award winning European social enterprise Archipelago and sits on University College Dublin's Innovation Academy board of studies. Additionally, he is the Dublin curator of the World Economic Forum Young Global Shapers. You can find out more about John at iamjohnegan.com or follow him on Twitter **@iamjohnegan**.

INTRODUCTION

"If you want something new, you have to stop doing something old."

Peter F. Drucker

FOR SOME TIME, discussion on the future of banking has been dominated by legislative reform and remunerative adjustments. There has been a laboured debate on whether the banking industry is a broken arm of civic governance or the great evil of our time. Bankers have been castigated for being sociopathic megalomaniacs, governments for being recklessly antisocial and citizens for being needlessly irresponsible. But little has been said at all about the future structure of the industry, its players and the inevitable influence of technology on the way we interact with finance and each other.

We have watched over the last half a decade as banks worked tirelessly towards restabilising normality in an industry artificially sustained, obdurately oblivious to the reality that whatever the new normal happens to be it is very unlikely that it will entertain the archaic, inflexible and regressive presence of retail banks without substantial and permanent change.

That change will see the most significant shift in corporate capacity since the Second World War. Stalwarts of the old guard will fall by the wayside, too inflexible to evolve, too scared to try. New players and ideas will emerge, many from the start-up community but mostly from adjacent industries. Those banks that survive will be entirely different entities. We will witness the rise of the networked bank, the rise of the platform, the rise of the user and, ultimately, the accelerated demise of the traditional notions of banks and banking.

The decline of the neighbourhood retail bank will give rise to a new world order of banking protagonists. Technology will fill the experiential vacuum between banks, deposits legislation will be circumvented, and networks will dictate industry winners and losers. The current protagonists of the banking sector are behemoths whose huge power stems from industry barriers to entry, permission-based access to credit and personal deposits; characteristics which the internet is systematically sidestepping. Peer-to-peer lending, crowd funding, digital wallets and currencies, payments technology and networked banking will redefine an antiquated industry.

Over the next two decades, a technologically enabled cohort of leaders made up of the more dynamic of the old world banks, adjacent industries and start-ups will rise to prominence. Banking will be mobile, money will be digital, branches will be exceptions and deposits will be an unnecessary balance sheet risk. Banking will be diversified, products customisable, service reviewable advice will be crowd sourced and ultimately banks will be *user-driven, open* and *networked.*

THE WHAT: USER-FOCUSED BANKING

"It is not by augmenting the capital of the country, but by rendering a greater part of that capital active and productive than would otherwise be so, that the most judicious operations of banking can increase the industry of the country."

Adam Smith

Traditionally, banks derive an income from arbitrage transactions; buying money from one market at one rate and selling it to another market at another rate without adding any value in between. Legislative, technological and economic barriers have heretofore prevented competitors from reducing the transactional friction of that intermediary margin. But rapid deployment of mobile devices and improvements in internet infrastructure have reduced the technological impediments to competitors interested in selling into the banking space.

The incremental redundancy of conventional retail banks will parallel the incremental adoption of alternative, technology enabled, user focused banking models. The networked bank is a platform-based bank focused on users rather than customers. It's a conceptual banking structure where individual banks act as intermediaries, facilitating capital flow between users rather than acting as a market maker or wholesaler. Instead of accepting deposits and giving loans, the networked bank focuses on coordinating loans between their enormous user-base.

To be clear, the networked bank is not a conventional bank in the sense that it buys and sells credit. Instead, it is effectively a technology company providing users with the mechanism needed to buy and sell credit independently and by doing so it reduces the friction of capital trade.

The networked bank does not accept deposits at a market set rate. In fact, it doesn't pay you at all for deposits. You lodge your savings at 0% and the networked bank provides you with the tools to create your own loans at whatever terms you want. The data available to banks, including credit history, savings, credit card activity, salary, expenses, etc., allows them to create an accurate risk profile of every user. That profile then dictates a specific rate that users can borrow at.

When you, the user, deposit your savings with the bank you decide what you want to earn and what you're willing to risk with your savings. The bank breaks up your deposit into hundreds of thousands of units and coordinates a series of tranched micro loans based on your risk appetite across a huge variety of borrowers, resulting in varying rates of return, completely defined by you, the user.

Your micro loan is amalgamated with thousands of other micro loans to produce the total loan amount required by the borrower who is paying a preset rate. Depending on the return you required your loan gets prioritised by tranches, so if the borrower can't pay all of their interest payment you the user have already established the priority of your repayment. If they can't pay the loan back then the impact to you the lender is negligible because it was such a small amount of the total you lent.

You get to create your own investment products and the bank earns an intermediary fee. The enormous user base means portfolio diversification is almost perfect and risk, return and price can be predicted with extremely high accuracy. So the user who wants to create a product that earns an expected 8% return with a 5% guaranteed return over one year can create that product, and so on. The product range is infinite and completely at the discretion of the user, resulting in a far more liquid capital environment.

Banks already have most of what they need to build this type of platform: credibility, brand awareness, capital, government support, millions of customers already on board, terabytes of data on every customer, and billions of annual transactions. The one major change that will be required is transitioning customers to users in a significant shift in perception – banks have millions of customers, all operating as autonomous entities, all buying and selling credit from and to a single institution, but never interacting with each other. To be clear, this is not about *social* interaction, but networked interaction; an amalgamation of resources for the betterment of the market. Social is about sharing, networks are about efficiency.

THE WHY: BELIGERENTLY BROKEN BANKING

"When the biggest, richest, glassiest buildings in town are the banks, you know that town's in trouble."

Edward Abbey

The great delinquency of modern banking is that its function often runs contrary to its requirements. That is to say banking is the only industry that directly connects the administrative burden of statecraft with the civic burden of governance. A nation, and ergo a government, requires banking to provide liquidity within an economy. The often recalcitrant populace, however, do not typically concern themselves with the macroeconomic liquidity requirements of the nation state.

The average citizen, the *individual*, does require access to wealth security, advisory and credit on a regular basis. The role of the banking industry becomes that of an intermediary, balancing the financial sustenance requirements of the individual with the liquidity needs of the nation, or the *collective*. Banking must operate within the constraints of the legislation governing it and obviously when a nation legislates, it does so to maximise value for the country as a whole, that is the collective and never the individual.

For the longest time the legislation governing banking did not act as an obstacle to servicing the demands of the individual. Conventionally, legislation delivered national liquidity by reinforcing public trust in the banking mechanism. Governments legislated that banks needed a licence to accept deposits, must maintain specific liquidity ratios, must protect customer data and must have new products licenced by independent authorities.

Consequently banks gained more and more customers, becoming more and more integral to the economy, thereby making deposits less and less risky and accordingly interest rates got lower and lower, reducing the friction of trade in an economy and increasing the pace of development (remember, money lending rates are far higher than bank interest and can often have significant associated health and moral hazard). In effect, cheap interest rates meant easier access to funds, more stuff was bought and sovereign wealth grew exponentially, bringing technology, culture, education and society along with it. Customers demand, banks supply and the free market is satiated.

However, when a country elects to artificially support the banking sector through the injection of unearned capital it effectively impedes the function of the free market. It creates what could be seen as an authorised, orchestrated oligopoly, a government controlled cartel. What we have seen over the last five years is a significant divergence in the needs of the individual and the collective. The needs of the individual have started to run contrary to the needs of the group. What's good for the goose is no longer good for the gander.

National need, specifically liquidity, required governments to intercede to ensure the survival of a system which had been proved to be cataclysmically unsustainable. The government, the representative of the collective, concluded that a bad system, artificially maintained and altered over time through legislation, was better than no system or a blank slate. They accepted that growth would slow and even shrink, but nations would survive, peace and social order would be maintained and the collective would suffer the minimum aggregate discomfort.

The collective is the amalgamation of all expected utilities for all individuals with purchasing power and right to representation, particular to a single jurisdiction, living, dead or as yet unborn. Let's call the economic effect of this amalgamation of need and want the *collective market*. The collective, in the form of government, is expected and often obliged to hypothesise future requirements of the collective and establish provisions for them now. The individual, on the other hand, is not.

The millions of individuals who were suddenly excluded from the credit infrastructure – who no longer trusted their money was safe, who didn't believe the banks' advice, who didn't think banks' investments were astute, who thought that the lack of bank investment in technology was negatively impacting trade or merchants who's bank was no longer a safe or cheap guarantor – became impatient and began to look towards and create alternatives made possible by new technology. This is what we call the *free market*; the amalgamation of all unhindered active utilities for all individuals with any access to a particular marketplace at a particular point in time. It is wholly representative of an individual's commercially actionable desires at a particular moment.

In short, the free market is what all of us want as single entities together and the collective market is what all of us want together as a single entity. The divergence between the free and collective markets has been the catalyst for what will eventually be the end of banks and the reformation of banking.

The reason being that the individual is only ever concerned with the economics of today; the economics of their own personal survival. Neither sustaining the bad banks nor financial collapse is in the best interest of the individual, but in only one of these two scenarios is there a quantifiable pecuniary imposition on the individual in the form of higher taxes or public cut backs. The insinuation is that consequently the free market will look to develop alternative methods for satisfying customer need instead of paying for what they don't want, i.e. a bank bail out.

Banking in its current guise can no longer provide a critical mass of the consumer base with the services it requires in the way it requires so as to prevent alternatives being created. Enough of the base has been pushed outside of the net to legitimise the development of substitutes. From mobile payments in Kenya to credit card payment tool Square, the fringe are developing innovations that are far outstripping the capabilities of traditional banks.

The divergence between the collective market and the free market is what is causing a technological and social revolution in banking. It is forcing the seven traditional services of banking – lending, deposits, investment, trade, security, advice and distribution of currency – to evolve in a way that fully integrates technology and networks, as demonstrated by peer-to-peer lending, crowd sourced financial advice, digital wallets and digital currency. The seen services of banking are not changing, but how they are provided is changing and banks are going to have to change radically if they hope to be part of the new order.

HOW: BANKS, CARS AND FASTER HORSES

"If I had asked people what they wanted, they would have said faster horses."

Henry Ford

SYSTEMATIC INNOVATION VS. SYSTEMIC INNOVATION

Banks and the protagonists adjacent to the industry need to innovate in a significant and meaningful way. Innovation, however, is a foreign concept to a monopolistic industry. Banks don't know how to innovate. Banks endure.

Conventional, iterative innovation is not enough to survive in the banking space. Banks and adjacent players need to obliterate traditional bank paradigms and practices in favour of more efficient alternatives. Protagonists in the banking space need to innovate in a systemic, rather than systematic, way.

Systematic innovation is a process of continuous and incremental innovations along a company or industry-specific curve (industry innovation curve, IIC). The most significant impact a systematic innovation can have is to alter the trajectory of the IIC. Systematic innovations are nearly always focused on efficiency; think about improvements in camera film during the 1980s, cordless home phones in the 1990s, or blue-ray DVDs in the 2000s.

Systemic innovation, however, is a transitional innovation that moves a company or industry from one IIC to a new curve due to improvements in effectiveness and will often result in the obsolescence of the previous product; see digital cameras, mobile phones, Netflix or, in Henry Ford's case, the automobile. When Henry Ford mentioned faster horses, he didn't mean that customers should be excluded from the innovation process, just that the customer role in innovation lies specifically within the systematic innovation space. Ultimately, systemic innovation is the burden of the company and failure to deliver systemic innovation will invariably result in an organisation or industry's decline.

If an organisation focuses on customer data or sentiment when considering product or service innovations, they are immediately limiting themselves to the parameters of that particular product or service and the constraints of the company to deliver improvements.

Considering customer data and sentiment restricts an organisation to innovations of ideas and concepts that the uneducated customer thinks might be feasible and compatible with the way they live their life at this particular point in time. Customer data will not ideate on concepts that might be relevant or effective in three years from now, because customers are only concerned with now, never the next; it is the role of the organisation to be concerned with next. Ask a customer how they would improve their laptop and they might have said "make it lighter", "improve the screen" or "increase the storage", because they are all existing demands. It is unlikely that sentiment or user data would have suggested tablets, touch screens or cloud storage, as these are systemic shifts in the IIC, creating entirely new demands and making many old products redundant.

TOWARDS SYSTEMIC INNOVATION IN BANKING

Banking now finds itself in a position where banks have provided a small number of customer-led systematic innovations in the last decade in the form of online banking, self-service banking and mobile apps, but has fundamentally failed to deliver any systemic innovation. Banks have made the process of dealing with a bank more efficient but have failed to make banking more effective. If banks are to survive, they don't need faster horses; they need cars.

The first step towards systemic innovation in the banking sector is the very pronounced and deliberate philisophical transition from customers to users; the shift from vertical interaction to horizontal experience. The proliferation and acceptance of the internet means that banks are no longer the single mechanism of exchange between buyers and sellers of credit.

Conceptually, customers are individuals who buy from you; users on the other hand are individuals who buy through you. If your company buys in raw material and uses that material to produce a product by adding value, then you're likely to have customers. If your organisation buys a finished product from one market and sells it into another, then the only way you can add value is through a platform and consequently you should have users. Banks don't actually add value to credit, i.e. they don't fundamentally change or improve the credit they bought through deposits before selling it as loans, and accordingly they should be user-focused through platforms, not customer-focused through service. Banks shouldn't be trying to sell you anything, they should be trying to help you sell.

The problem with customer-focused banking is that banks will only provide a small range of products to a very large number of people, like someone selling Christmas trees, where there are a few different types of tree to suit everyone who comes looking. Banking is a utility; it's something we all need and because we all need it, there exists a staggeringly wide range of distinctive demands and risk profiles. The products and services that we actually want from a bank are the culmination of every other aspect of our life. This includes what we earn, what we eat, where we live, what we like, who we like, how we communicate, to who we communicate, how we perceive risk and reward, what we want, what we dream, what we fear; all of these factors combine to create a ultra-specific set of needs for a banking customer. No two customers are the same and yet we all get force fed the same narrow set of products!

Think of chocolate. I walk into a shop and I can choose from literally hundreds of different bars of chocolate to satisfy, what is in essence, a very simple need: hunger. Despite being a significantly smaller industry and of substantially less import (although this point has been argued in editing), the chocolate industry is far more understanding of customer need than banks are. Simply put, P2P banking, digital wallets, online payments and advisory all exist because someone wanted almonds in their Snickers.

A user-centric bank prioritises customisation as a matter of course. Sellers are given the freedom to create products however they see fit, as long as it meets the platforms' terms & conditions, thereby providing buyers with a much more comprehensive marketplace. Think of Amazon; Amazon sell their own products but complement that offering by letting anyone sell alongside them, creating a massively dynamic and broad marketplace. If I'm buying a book, I can choose from a range of prices, conditions, sellers, editions and versions, and Amazon's user reviews act as online quality control ensuring I'm educated and protected.

A user-focused bank can concentrate on maximising the amount of actual credit transactions by perfectly matching buyers and sellers through mobile, online, user-orientated platforms, and not by selling homogenous products to heterogeneous customers. A user-focused bank understands that traditional banks are intermediaries; they buy a product from one market and sell it into another without adding value. A user-focused bank understands that traditionally, barriers like legislation and capital outlay prevented alternatives but now technology is mitigating that problem. Ultimately, a user-focused bank acts as a conduit and charges you for providing the product, not for the product itself.

The conventional relationship between bank and customer is vertical, dictatorial and rooted in user-prompted interactions. Its whole mode of operation is geared toward selling as many products as possible, not towards selling as much credit as possible. It removes all power and choice from the customer and forces them to subscribe to a rigid, mass market approach when it's no longer necessary. It leaves a tremendous amount of capital on the table by mismatching and mis-selling to customers.

Why can't you log in to your bank account to request a loan at 6% for five years with a four-month moratorium and irregular payments because you're an extremely low credit risk? This single set of institutions is incapable of providing products which can satisfy the market to the point that alternatives are not both attractive and feasible. These alternatives will originate in two primary spaces; start-ups and adjacent industry.

THE WHO: KEEPING UP WITH THE JONESES

"Never innovate to compete, innovate to change the rules of the game."

David O. Adeife

ADJACENT INDUSTRIES – THE BLEEDING EDGE OF INNOVATION – THE FORCE THAT PULLS

Adjacent industries are industries peripheral to the core business of the constituent companies but capable of, or necessary to, reduce transaction friction. As the protagonists in adjacent industries grow, they usually begin to migrate vertically as well as horizontally. Traditionally, legislation prohibited and available technology prevented companies from moving vertically into the banking sector, but over the last decade we have seen the likes of Tesco and Toyota move into financing, Telephonica launched the money card and Google created a digital wallet and payments platform.

Given that the primary purpose of banking is to make it easier for us to buy and sell stuff, it appears increasingly likely that more of these large companies will target vertical acquisitions, allowing them to disintermediate financing where possible, creating a more fluid and controlled transaction experience. The likes of Google, Apple, IKEA, Amazon, Zynga and Vodafone all have the capabilities, the capital and the customers to expand vertically into the banking space.

Large companies are the primary innovative force within any industry, they have the greatest access to capital, talent and technology, and accordingly they are the force that pulls. This might seem anathema to what we have been encouraged to think since the start-up boom in the early 2000s, but it's worth bearing in mind that technology products can only make the transaction experience for other products more efficient. They do not, in and of themselves, create value. Pharmaceuticals, robotics, capital equipment, construction, communications, computers, telecoms companies, etc., all start small and can of course be innovative in their approach to business, but it's not until they are more substantial entities that they can invest the capital required to make significant leaps in product innovation.

START-UPS – THE BLEEDING EDGE OF TRENDS – THE FORCE THAT PUSHES

Start-ups on the other hand are the force that pushes, the force that prods, the force that prompts innovation within an industry. They are the harbingers of change, but like the pacesetter in a distance race they are rarely contenders in the medal hunt, usually having dropped out earlier in the contest, unable to compete with the elite. Despite what start-ups like to think about themselves, they are rarely innovative in any area other than design. They almost never have access to the business or technical skills of a larger company, but they do represent the bleeding edge of trends.

Start-ups are the direct responsive consequence of consumer demand. They are representative of opportunities that appear in the gaps when technologies in adjacent industries evolve at different paces and they are usually started by someone who has encountered a problem and found peers with similar problems. Start-ups can move fast – extremely fast. They can release multiple iterations of a product a year, refine it, redesign it and redevelop it, all in accordance with almost immediate customer feedback.

The problem with start-ups is that although they are fantastic indicators of industry migration they are rarely capable of fulfilling their potential and competing with the bigger players. For the thousands of start-ups that take on a problem, very few of them will be significant players. Many of them will be absorbed by larger companies or fail to scale. So while start-ups have a significant impact on the trajectory of an industry by virtue of the fact that they are phenomenal indicators of market trends, they are very rarely a competitive industry force.

THE OLD WORLD BANKS – THE EDGE THAT'S BLEEDING – THE FORCE THAT'S MOVED

As technology and regulation evolve, banking will be forced to change. What that change looks like will be defined primarily by consumer trends as represented by start-ups – the force that pushes, and innovation at large companies in adjacent industries – the force that pulls.

One thing looks almost certain: banks in their current form are unsustainable by every metric. If it wasn't for government support, most of the western world's banks would have been wiped out. So if many of the traditional banks' services will be more effectively delivered by start-ups and adjacent industries in the future, will there still be banks and what will they look like?

Many of the existing stalwarts will survive but only if they can adapt to both technological and legislative conditions. Government will legislate away traditional banks because no government can afford a repeat of the last five years. This will be made infinitely easier for the governments to do because of the emergence of new alternatives and opportunities for traditional banks to transition their business models into less potent organisations. The core of this transition will be the networked bank – a bank focussed on users not customers.

Customers resent being dependent on banks but feel like they have few alternatives. Compare that reality to the likes of Google, Facebook and Apple, all of them larger companies than most banks, whose users freely elect and enjoy their products despite an abundance of alternatives. We're not dependent on Google, Facebook or Apple, yet we choose to use them. These companies have learned to win by putting the platform first, and platforms have users not customers. They allow us the freedom to dictate the terms of the relationship and the flexibility and dynamism to tailor our own experience.

Banks, on the other hand, oblige us to select from a homogenous product offering, with little input, flexibility or discretion. They make it difficult to buy the products and are almost archaic in their distribution methods. Banks don't need branches because customers want them; customers want them because banks can't function without branches.

CONCLUSION: THE WHEN

"...With something so important, a deeper mystery seems only decent."

John Kenneth Galbraith

Facebook has over 1 billion users, over 300m people search Google in any 24-hour period and Apple sell more iPhones every day than there are babies born. The iPhone is six years old, just two years younger than Facebook and eight years younger than Google. Wells Fargo is the 23rd biggest bank in the world; it has 70m customers. It took them over 160 years to accumulate them.

Google's empire spans from cryogenics to space technology; they can fundamentally change the banking industry whenever they choose and if recent investments in peer-to-peer lenders are anything to go by, they have already decided. Conventional banks can no more compete with the smart networked platforms of the adjacent industries than horses could with the Model T.

There are no absolutes in any context, but there are extreme likelihoods, predictable dependencies and degrees of statistic confidence. Conventional retail banking is unsustainable, as banks themselves have demonstrated. The model is no longer compatible with technology, legislation, society or business and must change in accordance with this evolution. The networked bank is just the simplest most feasible transformation for a traditional bank. So, while not their only choice, it may be their only chance.

THE NEXT GENERATION FINANCE MEGATREND

BY BY ROBERT LEMPKA, THOMAS WINKLER AND MARC P. BERNEGGER

ABOUT THE AUTHORS

Robert Lempka is co-founder and co-manager of Next Generation Finance Invest AG (Switzerland) which invests in business models and technologies leading to more efficiency in financial markets. He led a consortium of investors in Gekko in November 2009 and actively supports the CEO in developing Gekko into a leading edge provider of financial services. Robert invested in companies like OANDA, ayondo and Brady. Robert was CEO of ABN AMRO marketindex and prior to that he held trading management positions at Goldman Sachs International and Dresdner Kleinwort.

Thomas Winkler is co-founder and investment manager at the listed investment company Next Generation Finance Invest AG (Switzerland) and is a business angel with a focus on tomorrow's financial industry. Before he started Next Generation Finance Invest he was CEO of ABN AMRO Switzerland and global head of private investor products at ABN AMRO in London.

Marc P. Bernegger is a serial entrepreneur, partner and co-manager of Next Generation Finance Invest AG (Switzerland). Before this he founded the party platform usgang.ch (which was sold to media company Axel Springer) and was the co-founder of amiando, which was awarded the title 'Global Technology Pioneer' by the World Economic Forum (WEF) and acquired by the business platform Xing. In

2010, Marc was voted 'Newcomer of the Year' by the Swiss ICT association. He holds a Master of Law from the University of Zürich.

INTRODUCTION

ORIGINALLY DEVELOPED BY the United States Department of Defense to network universities and other research facilities, the internet has spread across the entire globe in only a few short years. Its seemingly unlimited growth has already blurred the boundary between the virtual and real worlds, and how the digital revolution will develop in the future is hard to predict.

The changes in society as well as the economy caused by the internet and the digital revolution are practically unprecedented. Taking just one example of these changes, with digital content now available on mobile devices (such as smartphones like the Apple iPhone), for the first time billions of people across the planet have access to the same information at the same time – an entirely new phenomenon.

FUNDAMENTAL ECONOMIC CHANGES

The economy is a major area that has been affected by these developments. Indeed, the business world has never been affected by so many fundamental changes in such a short time. Professions that did not even exist ten years ago are now viewed as absolutely indispensable. Other professions that thrived for generations have either partially or completely disappeared.

At the same time, advances in technology have led to the sudden rise of companies providing products that were themselves only recently invented. In the space of only a few years, these companies have become multinational corporations with billions in turnover. Google, for example, was founded only 14 years ago by two students. Today, it is one of the largest companies in the world. It employs more than 53,000 workers and posted a profit of over $50 billion in 2012.

ADVANCES IN TECHNOLOGY AND THE INTERNET AS AN AGENT OF CHANGE

From brand new start-up companies to numerous innovations of existing products and businesses, advances in technology have reduced the barriers to entry to unprecedentedly low levels for new business models. As a result, the internet has completely revolutionised industries such as publishing and trade in recent years and in doing so has spawned multinational corporations such as eBay and Amazon.

Even if it is delayed by several years, there is little doubt the finance industry will experience a similar seismic shift and a change in existing value chains. This megatrend is in its early phases now, but it will affect the finance industry for many years to come.

The causes and driving factors of these changes include:

- The availability of fast data connections (broadband internet) used by many new web services.

- Smartphones allowing mobile and therefore uninterrupted access to the internet.

- Global network security standards essential for online transactions, particularly in the banking sector.

- A general loss of confidence in established banks caused or aggravated by the financial crisis. As a result, even large multinational financial firms with well-known names are no longer automatically viewed as more reliable than newer providers.

- Customers increasingly expect more flexible and transparent services from the financial sector. The decision to purchase a product is based more on the product itself than on the provider, meaning the importance of established financial institutions with high fixed costs is diminishing.

- More transparency in the so-called *financial services jungle*, with countless new online communities and comparison portals allowing consumers to better compare financial services and stay well-informed.

- As the generation of digital natives comes of age, new services are required to meet changing customer needs. This new generation of consumers with growing purchasing power demands constant access to services (on new devices such as smartphones and tablets), and is highly concerned with cost. In this environment, providers with slim and dynamic corporate structures offering clear customer benefits will have a decisive advantage. Price discrimination against private investors will no longer be accepted by these consumers.

Established financial institutions have mostly neglected to invest in future technologies in good years and now no longer have the financial resources for investment. That has created an opportunity for highly specialised providers of IT services ensuring cost-efficient product distribution.

THE DEMOCRATISATION OF THE FINANCIAL INDUSTRY

As other industries have seen in recent years, changes caused by the digital revolution lead to a democratisation of traditional businesses. The same will be true for the financial industry. Interactions are no longer exclusively between financial institutions and their customers, but also increasingly among the customers themselves (for example, social banking). Social networks such as Twitter and Facebook have created new kinds of interactions. In order to take advantage of the new opportunities created by these interactions, service providers have to accept they will not be control of this new dialogue (or perhaps more appropriately today, monologue) with consumers, which is an uncomfortable transition for them to face.

Very few financial institutions have reacted to these changes and many are intimidated by the risks involved in the changing information exchange from one-way communication to communication with many participants. Social media activities in banking are either nonexistent or very subdued, and often little more than token efforts. But the experience of other industries leaves no doubt that it is only a question of time before the financial industry will have to confront these changes, and that the internet will inevitably force it to be more democratic and more transparent.

INVESTMENT IN THE FINANCIAL SECTOR, 2.0

Despite the enormous opportunities it offers, it is astounding how few investors are familiar with internet-based business models in the financial industry. On the investor side, the concept of next generation finance business models (known as *finance 2.0*) has not received the attention it deserves given its potential for the financial sector. There are only a handful of angel investors active in early-phase financing (seed, venture and early-stage financing) of these models. Apart from Next Generation Finance Invest (www.nextgfi.com), there are no institutional investors with a dedicated focus on *finance 2.0* and *banking 2.0*.

This is because linking traditional, highly-regulated business models with cutting-edge, internet-based distribution models characterised by rapid growth is an enormous challenge. Finding common ground for these opposing models is a highly complex enterprise that requires profound expertise in the areas of finance, IT and online marketing.

OUTLOOK

As we have seen, banks and the financial industry are currently experiencing a painful transition process that will alter the sector to an unprecedented degree. Although these fundamental changes may not occur overnight, and could take years depending on the specific area and market, transformation is inevitable.

Innovative approaches, cutting-edge technologies and slimmer business models may allow new market participants to eclipse established institutions in some areas.

NEXT GENERATION FINANCE AS A MEGATREND

In the future, disintermediation in banking will increase and new actors will dominate certain areas of the financial markets. This trend is already a major factor in forex (consumer currency trading). The company OANDA (www.oanda.com) is one of the pioneers in this area. The increasing influence of new models is certain to affect other areas of the financial industry as well.

The use of *wrappers* such as contracts for difference (CFDs) could play a fundamental role here, in breaking traditional value chains. CFDs are synthetic financial products offered mainly on electronic trading platforms (such as www.gekkomarkets.com) at a low price.

A CFD of Apple shares, for example, exactly mirrors the performance of those shares without requiring the shares to be actually purchased. That means the buyer does not pay any order fees, exchange fees or any other type of commission. The result is an incredibly low-cost direct business between the trading platform and the customer that leaves banks and exchanges entirely out of the equation. CFD positions can be either leveraged or unleveraged and can also be purchased in fractions (for example 0.1 or 0.5 Apple shares).

These efficient, flexible and low-cost wrappers could facilitate many emerging business models, such as social trading, and will play an important role in financial markets in the future. This is especially true in asset management, an area currently dominated by companies with outdated structures and high fees.

Internet-based approaches in finance that take advantage of new technology – such as P2P lending, crowdfunding, personal finance management and social trading – are still in their infancy. Only time will tell how quickly and successfully these business models will establish themselves.

Stronger regulation will hinder the creation of new products that lack transparency and carry high margins, maintain financial institution incomes at low levels, and make cuts on the cost side necessary. The new product manager motto will be "a tenth of the price with a tenth of the staff" – something practically unthinkable for established financial institutions with their inflexible structures and high fixed costs. New players in the market will dedicate themselves to breaking existing value chains. By relying on slim, low-cost structures adapted to the industry's changed requirements, these new providers will be able to take advantage of opportunities that never existed before.

Certainly, established financial service providers are not idly standing by while these changes occur. In some new markets they are establishing a presence by forming product partnerships with emerging, innovative and technology-driven companies. But these partnerships are usually not prominently positioned, and are often just half-hearted attempts to protect themselves in case these business models actually catch on and become established.

Financial service providers are increasingly relying on outsourcing to ensure their piece of this potentially enormous pie, but that means they risk being left behind if massive changes arrive too quickly.

It remains to be seen what opportunities this environment will offer new providers, and whether these new business models will prove sustainable and lasting. What is not in doubt is that established financial service providers will come under increasing pressure to reduce their margins and costs. This will in turn force them to take aggressive action in response to the fundamental changes in the financial market created by next generation finance business models.

FINANCIAL REPRESSION –
IS SOMEONE BATTING FOR YOU?

BY AKSHAY KAPOOR AND SARAH BRYLEWSKI

ABOUT THE AUTHORS

Akshay Kapoor is Business & Product Development Director at Gekko Global Markets. As a board member, among other things he is responsible for transforming the product offering and driving the strategic agenda. Before Gekko, Akshay had a long track record of building cross asset sales and trading businesses with leading global investment banks. He is passionate about democratising finance and is proud that Gekko is leading the charge to return power to customers.

Sarah Brylewski is Head of Germany, Gekko Global Markets.

INTRODUCTION

"Concentrated power is not rendered harmless by the intentions of those who create it."

Milton Friedman

"Hell isn't merely paved with good intentions; it's walled and roofed with them. Yes, and furnished too."

Aldous Huxley

THE LAST 100 years have transformed human society. Developed nations created a lot of wealth, significantly improving the quality of life of their citizens and reducing inequality. Huge advances were made by states in providing education, health, security and fulfilling their people's aspirations. New economic giants like China and India have emerged and hundreds of millions have been lifted out of poverty.

Political freedoms have grown, helped in a large measure by globalisation and the rapid advance of communication technology and social media. Technology has been harnessed to solve a lot of problems and improve lives. Of course, progress has its costs and a lot of the benefits we have reaped have taken their toll on the environment. But hopefully we can bring human ingenuity to bear and resolve some of these issues.

Our focus in this article is to explore whether one very important aspect of this progress – financial well-being and security – can continue into the future.

What are people up against and who can they depend on?

THE AGE OF FINANCIAL REPRESSION

When Alan Greenspan stated in the early 2000s that he would rather let bubbles grow and burst and then clean up the mess (by blowing bigger bubbles), he set the tone for a reversal of the steady increase in financial well-being that we saw in the last century. He and his successor Ben Bernanke – supported by policy makers and central bankers across the world – started the age of Financial Repression. Ever since, well-meaning central banks and governments have been printing money like there is no tomorrow, egged on by economists and multilateral organisations. We don't talk about QE 1, 2 or 3 now. We talk of QE-infinity. We don't raise our eyebrows when the Bank of

England governor misses the only explicit target (inflation at 2%) in his job description two-thirds of the time over five years. We just remove the inconvenience of the target!

The intentions were good – print money, that will lower interest rates, people will borrow and spend, and businesses will invest. That will kick-start growth, creating more jobs and prosperity. How has it worked out? The majority of people in developed countries are worse off. Real incomes have fallen and inequality has grown to record levels. It is estimated that the wealthiest 1% now control almost 40% of the world's wealth and those worth more than $5m control 25% of the world's wealth. The biggest driver of wealth in developed countries has been financial markets but this wealth has been heavily concentrated. That is no surprise of course. As the printing presses churn out money, it somehow sticks to the hands of those closest to the presses.

Our money buys much less than it did ten years ago; houses are much more expensive and incomes have not kept pace. If you have a lot financial and real assets, such as stock bought at 2009 lows, property and commodities, then this has worked out well for you. But the vast majority do not. Inflating away vast debts and off-balance-sheet government entitlement liabilities is now accepted policy. That is why money printing has failed to create jobs and growth but has become a recipe for financial repression.

At the same time that savers are being penalised by negative real interest rates, they cannot depend upon the state for fulfilling its medical care and pension obligations when they retire. They have no choice but to take charge of their own financial future. However, the odds are stacked against them. Large mainstream financial institutions are not configured to deliver value to small firms and individual clients. Institutional and ultra-high net worth clients get the best service, information, advice and execution, while the smaller investor has to contend with high fees, shoddy service and indifferent performance. With fees, charges and taxes, a *good* return of 7% to 8% per annum on a managed fund can swiftly be reduced to 2% to 3%. With many active funds failing to consistently beat the index investors cannot afford the status quo.

A CHALLENGE TO THE STATUS QUO

Fortunately the status quo is being challenged. Till now financial services have been shielded from the shift of power to the consumer that transformed industries like retail and media, but that is changing.

As financial services go through a painful transition, innovative new players are challenging the established behemoths in all sectors of the industry. These challengers are democratising finance. As the new kids on the block they are forced to make the most of tight resources and small marketing budgets. Therefore, they have to focus on the customer in order to survive.

They have to identify a pressing need and fulfill it by providing a product that solves important problems for customers. In order to reach as many clients as possible with their small marketing budgets they need to use word of mouth and social media. To succeed in these channels you need credibility with clients. That means the product has to deliver what it says on the label, have no nasty surprises and treat customers with respect, empathy and complete transparency.

As an example, in the asset management, retail trading and investment space, we at Gekko Global Markets are batting for our clients. We believe this is especially important in the current time of financial repression and in an industry which is completely undemocratic – an industry that treats institutional and retail investors so differently. Our goal is to change the financial services landscape, drive innovation and to create a level playing field.

One important part of doing this is to significantly reduce costs and improve access. If we want to make the private investor's life better it is necessary to take a closer look at the charges a typical retail investor would face when investing in equities or funds bought through a high street bank, online fund or share specialist. It should come as no surprise that it is not a great situation for the small investor. Nearly 30% of the profit a private investor makes has to be paid away as fees to fund marketers, advisors, brokers and institutions. Then of course investors have to bear losses themselves. With interest rates at historical lows and asset prices at all-time highs, investors cannot afford to give away such large swathes of performance.

More importantly, they actually need performance to begin with! So, do investors get performance from traditional funds? Interestingly enough, research shows that investors who avoid funds that charge a performance fee usually improve their returns. This is the finding of a study carried out by the rating agency Scope.

Scope's analysts compared the performance of almost 8000 funds and found over a time frame of five years that funds without performance-based compensation outperformed their peers who did charge performance fees by 1.9 percentage points per year. That is almost 10% over five years. The reason could be that performance fees for fund managers tend to incentivise fund managers in the wrong way and encourage them to take too much risk as they share the upside but not the downside.

Other fees have names that hardly fit into today's web enabled, hi-tech world, such as Urgent Bank Fees, Duplicate Statement Fees, Account Closure and Inactive Account Fees. These names have the sound of an old world, crusted structures and outdated technology. When you think that around 80% of all fund managers underperform their benchmark index, it needs some generosity to feel like paying away a big portion of your investment returns as additional charges for the fund.

As the world changes there is hope for the fund industry. In times where most product brochures are downloaded from the internet instead of taken away from a branch of a local bank, the industry saves a tremendous amount of marketing budget. In times where most newspapers struggle with advert booking clients, at least less money for print adverts has to be spent. Costs can be saved and private investors have to challenge the fund and banking industries to reduce product costs and commissions. Otherwise the industry will keep taking from customers what it can get away with.

DEMOCRATISING THE FINANCE INDUSTRY

That is why we are are trying to democratise the retail trading and investing space. This means creating affordable, transparent and accessible products for a large mass of clients – the private investors. Let's look at the definition of democracy:

> "Democracy is based on the freedom of the individual, guarantees the equality of the individual and puts any kind of action on a voluntary basis."

Therefore, democracy in the financial industry can only work if investors and customers are willing to change their investment habits and if they are open to innovation. Customer support and buy-in is essential to bring about change.

With the support of customers we should strive for nothing less than the complete democratisation of the financial industry. Openness, transparency and direct clear communication are not necessarily values that are associated with the traditional financial sector. This industry is in general still very conservative and is not willing to change and freshen up. That leaves a service, product, communication and innovation gap that can be, will be and is being filled by new, agile businesses that are solving real problems for clients.

At Gekko we are passionately committed to empowering clients and helping them achieve their financial goals. We have turned the UK spread betting tax advantage to our clients' favour and made it an instrument of long-term investing rather than just day trading. Using our revolutionary variable margin offering our clients can invest in any stock, asset class and market *completely tax free*. This is exactly the same as investing in stocks or shares with a broker but without the costs of stamp duty, dividend tax or capital gains tax. We charge a fraction of the fees of a managed account or fund and are at least as competitive as a discount broker. So we have created an offering that allows investment in any asset class at a fraction of the cost of traditional channels and which is completely tax free. *This is a no brainer and a direct response to financial repression.*

One of our biggest innovations is in the social trading space. With our group company ayondo we are creating a way for all kinds of investors and traders to democratically select the best traders/money managers from a large global pool and follow their trading activity proportionally with zero slippage and negligible costs by linking their account to them.

We don't think social trading is just providing an avenue for people to learn from each other, though that is an important part of it. We strongly believe that the most important part is to break down the barriers for highly talented but small managers to access assets under management and for small investors to access and get small amounts of money managed by the best, not necessarily largest, fund managers and traders. We are democratising the asset management industry.

Gekko Global Markets is the core of Next Generation Finance Group. The network of Next Generation Finance Invest is unique in the way disruptive business models meet innovative technologies in the financial sector. Together we are creating an ecosystem of innovative alternatives to traditional advice, product and execution at a fraction of the cost. And we are not alone. The industry is bubbling with activity.

If investors want to protect themselves from financial repression they will have to challenge their comfort zones and current ways of investing. They need to question the cost and value of traditional products and advice; they need to question the expertise of the *experts*; they need to take advantage of the new players. Above all, they need to start batting for themselves.

BITCOIN – A PROMISE OF FREEDOM

BY LUZIUS MEISSER

ABOUT THE AUTHOR

Luzius Meisser is a computer scientist currently pursuing a masters degree in economics. He co-founded secure online storage service Wuala. He is partner at Zeeder.ch – a business angel club focussing on internet startups – and teaches object-oriented programming at the Swiss University of Applied Sciences and Arts (FHNW).

INTRODUCTION

BITCOIN IS AN internet currency and payment platform that has recently gained remarkable traction in the media. In this article I will describe its core characteristics, perform a SWOT (strength, weaknesses, opportunities, threats) analysis, and shed light on its cypherpunk anarcho-capitalist philosophy.

The main trump card of bitcoin is its independence and the absence of central control, allowing it to explore opportunities in finance much more freely than any other platform. Bitcoin embodies a promise of freedom in a world paralysed by risk-aversion.

WHAT IS BITCOIN?

Bitcoin is a digital currency and payment system. Since its inception in 2008, it has enjoyed increasing popularity, with two spikes in its price in 2011 and 2013 due to an avalanche of press attention.[1] Its exchange rate grew from $0.10 in January 2011 to $100 in summer 2013, with a high of $260 in April 2013 when media attention peaked. Figure 1 shows how 'bitcoin' has grown as a search term on Google since January 2009.

Figure 1 – 'bitcoin' on Google Trends[2]

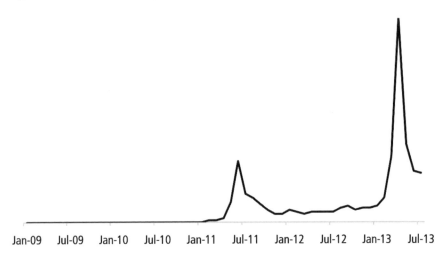

Jan-09   Jul-09   Jan-10   Jul-10   Jan-11   Jul-11   Jan-12   Jul-12   Jan-13   Jul-13

Bitcoins are freely transferable, divisible and secure. Yet this alone does not make them special. Anyone skilled in the art could create a computer system that keeps track of user accounts and their balances in a virtual currency and start selling units of this invented currency to gullible users. What sets bitcoin apart from previous systems is its decentralised nature. There is no centralised entity that controls bitcoin.

I will not discuss how bitcoin works technically. However, the following technical properties of bitcoin are relevant:

- Unlike other currencies, bitcoin is not backed by the rule of law, but by technology. Even if all legal systems collapse, bitcoin could still function as long as the internet exists and there are people willing to use it. For the avoidance of doubt, bitcoin is of course still subject to the law, even if it does not depend on it.

- Its decentralised and robust nature makes bitcoin hard to control or regulate.

- Bitcoin enjoys cryptographically strong property guarantees. If stored right, it is impossible to take away bitcoins against their owner's will.[3]

- As of summer 2013, there are 11m bitcoins in circulation and new ones are minted at a rate of 25 bitcoins every ten minutes. This rate will decline over time according to a predefined schedule, limiting the total amount of bitcoins that will ever be in circulation to 21m.

- Transactions are anonymous, but public. Anyone can have as many bitcoin addresses (comparable to numbered bank accounts) as desired and anyone owning such an address can freely send bitcoins to any other address. Every transaction ever executed is stored in a publicly accessible archive.

- In order to send someone bitcoins, the sender needs to be online, but not the recipient. There are also mechanisms to exchange bitcoins offline, but they require the two involved parties to trust each other.

- Transactions can be executed within seconds, but take up to an hour to be confirmed. Until confirmed, there is a slight and gradually diminishing chance of a transaction not being accepted by the network (e.g. due to the bitcoins being spent concurrently in two separate transfer attempts, a so-called *double-spend*).

- All transactions are executed and verified by thousands of computers in parallel – with an elaborate scheme in place to resolve inconsistencies by majority vote, whereas votes are weighted by computing power. Anyone's computer can take part in this system. Transaction fees are distributed among the participants of the bitcoin network as an incentive to contribute computing power. Until the limit of 21m bitcoins is reached, the newly minted bitcoins are handed out along with the transaction fees.

- Transaction fees are very low as there are many competing participants in the network. The currently recommended fee is 0.001 bitcoins, which is worth about $0.10.[4] In fact, it is better described as a tip than a fee. *Tip* originally stood for 'to insure promptness' and this is exactly what it does: the larger the transaction fee, the bigger the incentive to process a transaction and the more quickly it gets processed.

- Bitcoin has no underlying asset – just like conventional currencies.[5] There is no one that guarantees a value. The exchange rate is determined by supply and demand on the market.

Bitcoin is already accepted by thousands of businesses[6] and has an active community of developers, traders, enthusiasts and activists. Good resources for further information about bitcoin are: the bitcoin website (bitcoin.org), market research firm Genesis Block (thegenesisblock.com), the bitcoin forum (bitcointalk.org), the Bitcoin Foundation (bitcoinfoundation.org) and the bitcoin subreddit (reddit.com/r/bitcoin).

For charts and pricing information, I recommend Bitcoin Charts for historic charts (bitcoincharts.com/charts/mtgoxUSD); Bitcoinity for real-time market charts (bitcoinity.org/markets); Blockchain.info (a wallet service with a great charts function); and Mt.Gox market data, which is in the style of Bloomberg (bitcoin.clarkmoody.com). Popular sites to trade bitcoins include: Mt.Gox (mtgox.com); Local Bitcoins, for trading with people in your area (localbitcoins.com); Bitcoin.de, a German market place; and Bitstamp (bitstamp.net).

STRENGTHS

Bitcoin's first key strength is its decentralised architecture and absence of central control, which enables it to serve as an independent and open payment platform. The vast implications of this are explored in the opportunities and threats section.

A second significant strength are the strong property rights built on proven cryptographic methods. If stored correctly, no one can take your bitcoins against your will – not even indirectly through inflation, as often happens with fiat currencies. Bitcoin neither relies on the rule of law nor on the integrity of its operators. Its robust technology and the internet is all bitcoin needs to function.

As a third important strength, bitcoin is technologically sound and its core protocol can only be changed if there is a wide consensus among all stakeholders that such a change is necessary and good. This makes bitcoin a reliable platform to build on.

Further strengths are minimal fees and fast international transfers. The astonishing part about the fast transfers is not so much the speed of a bitcoin transfer, but its traditional competitors being extremely slow, with international wire transfers often taking a day or more to complete. The low fees are a consequence of its decentralised architecture and the resulting competition among transaction processors (known as *miners*).

WEAKNESSES

Bitcoin's strength of being decentralised and hard to control is also a weakness. It makes the bitcoin system very slow to adapt to change. When the market or regulation calls for changes to be made to the core of bitcoin, it is almost impossible to get them through. A majority of stakeholders such as core developers and large mining pools, which both are known to be very conservative about change, need to be convinced.

Another weakness and direct consequence of its decentralisation is that there is no entity with a concentrated and strong interest in promoting bitcoin. Sometimes enthusiasts pay for bitcoin ads out of altruism, but that is no replacement for a concerted marketing effort of a company that directly owns a product and reaps all the marketing returns for itself.

The same applies to the development of bitcoin. Like other open-source projects bitcoin depends on altruistic contributors that are attracted to it out of genuine interest and not for monetary reasons. This results in another weakness shared with other open-source projects: since it is much more rewarding to solve demanding core challenges most developers focus on those, neglecting user-friendliness.

What is also often considered a weakness is the fact that like cash, bitcoin is agnostic on laws and morality. It just works – regardless of the purposes it is used for. This is a trait typical of infrastructure technologies and it is also exhibited by the internet itself.

Furthermore, bitcoin is often criticised for being deflationary by design as its supply is limited. There is no central bank that can adjust money supply to the needs of the economy. A related weakness of bitcoin is its extreme volatility. Changes in value of more than 10% per day are not uncommon, forcing vendors to add a safety margin to quoted prices and immediately sell earned bitcoins for traditional units of account on receipt.

OPPORTUNITIES

There are various opportunities for bitcoin, both as a currency and as a payment system. Richard Falkvinge, founder of the Swedish Pirate Party, is so convinced about bitcoin that he announced he had invested all his savings and all he could borrow into bitcoin back in 2011. In his analysis of key drivers, he identified unlawful trade, international trade, merchant trade and investments.[7] I have chosen a different way of slicing bitcoin's opportunities and added a fifth category called 'Extensions'.

The five categories of opportunities I have identified are:

1. Traditional online payments
2. Offline payments
3. Micro-payments
4. Store of wealth
5. Extensions

1. TRADITIONAL ONLINE PAYMENTS

The most straightforward opportunity is in online payments. Today's most popular means of payment on the web is credit card, which has not improved much in the past 20 years and which is prone to fraud. Another popular system is PayPal, but it suffers from similar problems and is unpopular among merchants.[8]

Furthermore, the credit card market is a dysfunctional oligopoly. With typical interchange fees of 2%, credit cards can significantly hurt profits of a merchant that operates with low margins. At a margin of 5%, a credit card fee of 0.9% eats away almost a fifth of a merchant's profits. The European commission recently decided to finally take action and to limit credit card fees by law,[9] a measure that is only necessary when Adam Smith's famous invisible hand fails due to lack of competition. Many payment startups have tried to revolutionise the online payment market in the past and failed, PayPal being a notable exception.

Bitcoin's unique strength in this market is its credible guarantee of independence. This is what makes open source systems like Linux so successful: corporations can build on it without being afraid of vendor lock-in. In the online world, bitcoin is the first to offer such independence, giving it a role comparable to cash in the offline world. If the strategic interest of gaining independence from credit cards and PayPal is large enough, we can expect continuous adoption of bitcoin.

The first places to adopt bitcoin will be those who suffer the most from the current system. For example, in 2010, in a coordinated effort, credit card companies including PayPal and Bank of America froze all ongoing payments to controversial whistle-blowing site WikiLeaks without legal necessity and without prior warning, preventing WikiLeaks from receiving donations exactly when it had the most press attention and the most willing donors.

It took WikiLeaks three years of legal disputes to regain the ability to accept donations via credit card.[10] Meanwhile, they received over 3700 bitcoins – worth around $370,000 – in donations on their public donation address, with an unknown additional amount donated to non-public addresses by more privacy-concerned donors. Another company that chose to embrace bitcoin after suffering from legally doubtful sanctions is Mega.[11]

An example of a web shop that chose bitcoin as its payment system in order to avoid interchange fees is the American electronics retailer BitcoinStore (bitcoinstore.com). It is worth noting that the high volatility of bitcoin limits its benefit when used as a payment system. As bitcoin matures and volatility decreases, more shops like BitcoinStore could spawn. Low volatility is a necessary precondition for the benefits of low fees to fully flourish.

As long as volatility stays high, bitcoin primarily makes sense to businesses with high margins and to those in grey areas that live in fear of random sanctions from traditional payment services. Examples are the aforementioned WikiLeaks, drug marketplace Silk Road, adult sites and online gambling. SatoshiDice (satoshidice.com), a bitcoin gambling site, was recently acquired for 126,315 bitcoins, or about $11.5m. Rumours are that the buyer was the owner of popular poker site PKR, fuelling hopes that he might want to adopt bitcoin on a wider scale.[12]

To conclude, there is a big opportunity for bitcoin in markets that seek alternatives to the current payment systems, be it out of fear from sanctions or out of frustration with high fees. However, the latter driver cannot fully unfold as long as bitcoin stays highly volatile.

2. OFFLINE PAYMENTS

A second opportunity is offline payments. Although there are already a number of restaurants and stores that accept bitcoins, they are not expected to become widespread in the near future. The main drivers for offline payments at the moment are ideology – accepting bitcoin out of philosophical conviction – and marketing – accepting bitcoin to gain attention.

For most offline payments, cash is more comfortable than bitcoin. One exception is large volumes: carrying a million in cash requires a suitcase, whereas a million in bitcoins can be kept on a small memory card. Furthermore, there is an increasing number of countries with restrictions on cash transactions. For example, cash transactions above a certain size are illegal in Italy (€1000), Spain (€2500) and France (€3000). Here, bitcoin could fill a gap. But overall, I only see limited potential in offline payments due to competition from traditional cash.

3. MICRO-PAYMENTS

Another opportunity for bitcoin is in micro-payments. For a developer of a website or online game, it is trivial to accept bitcoins; it is a suitable technology to serve as in-game currency to buy power-ups or other in-game gadgets. However, a critical factor for this to be successful is bitcoin adoption among gamers, which has not happened as yet. On iOS devices, there is the additional handicap of Apple not allowing any payment service other than their own, with which they charge a hefty margin of 30% on all payments. Nonetheless, a hugely popular game – such as MineCraft – using bitcoin could serve as a catalyst for others to adopt.

A service that successfully uses bitcoin for micropayments is BitcoinTip, which allows users of the popular reddit forum to send each other small monetary rewards for insightful comments.[13] To do this users reply to a comment with "bitcointip 0.001 BTC confirm".

4. STORE OF WEALTH

There is an opportunity for bitcoin to be used as a store of wealth. Here, user-friendliness is secondary. All that counts is the ability to act as a secure and reliable store of value over time. As bitcoin is still young, confidence in its long-term value is limited. But for every year of existence without major problems, the likelihood that bitcoin is here to stay increases. Right now, betting on bitcoin still being around in 2020 takes courage. Assuming continued success, betting in 2020 that it will still be around in 2030 is much less risky. In other words, the number of features and the adoption as a means of payment are secondary for this opportunity to materialise. Additionally, bitcoin gains in attractiveness with decreasing volatility. This helps to explain why, in the past, some of the best times to invest in bitcoin were during extended periods of relatively stable prices.

As a rough estimate of how valuable bitcoin can become as a store of wealth, consider bills worth 1000 Swiss francs – not the most popular store of wealth, but neither will bitcoin be any time soon. Currently, there are 33 billion CHF of these bills in circulation,[14] with many residing outside Switzerland. Assuming that two-thirds of these bills are used as a store of value and assuming a comparable potential for bitcoin, this would translate into a value of $1000 for each of the 21m bitcoins.[15] This illustrates the impact that bitcoin becoming a somewhat popular store of wealth could have on its exchange rate.

Bitcoin is sometimes also compared to gold since both can be held as a hedge against extreme events and both just sit there and are valuable, without providing a dividend. However, unlike gold today, bitcoin is used for payments, which creates increasing demand as the bitcoin economy grows. Thus, holding bitcoins allows someone to participate in its growth. This makes owning bitcoins comparable to owning a share of the bitcoin economy.

5. EXTENSIONS

The innovative part of bitcoin is its proof-of-work protocol.[16] Bitcoin uses that protocol to keep track of who owns what amount of bitcoins. On an abstract level, the system can be seen as a very reliable and secure database suitable for storing small units of data.

One class of extensions can be based on the idea of coloured coins, which can be used to track possession of items.[17] For example, a restaurant could declare that it gives a meal to whoever pays with a particular bitcoin (or a fraction of a bitcoin) – regardless of the actual value of that bitcoin. That way, this bitcoin becomes a freely transferable voucher for a meal at that restaurant.

Alternatively, one could use coloured coins to enable trading of shares by declaring that a particular bitcoin represents all shares of a company and that dividends will be paid out proportionally to the addresses that hold fractions of this bitcoin once per year. As all transactions are public, it is easy to determine where to send the dividends. That way, bitcoin could act as an anonymous and secure directory of registered shares. One could even use this mechanism to perform cryptographically secure, yet anonymous, votes at the general assembly.

A third example would be to add a cryptographic lock to a car that is connected to the internet. As the ownership of a bitcoin can be securely verified, the lock could be programmed such that the car could only be started by the verified and current owner of a particular bitcoin. That way, that bitcoin becomes a token of car ownership and one could transfer ownership of the car simply by transferring that particular *coloured* coin.

Another class of extensions is enabled by the payment scripts bitcoin is designed to support (they are not fully activated yet to minimise complexity and risks). These scripts allow for more complex transactions, for example escrow services, transactions that require multiple signatures, timed transactions, and transactions that are bound to certain conditions such as the occurrence of a verifiable event.

All in all, there is enormous potential for clever extensions. Bitcoin truly shines as a platform in this regard and extensions might bring a few interesting surprises in the coming years. To precisely foresee these applications would be as hard as foreseeing Twitter in 1995.

THREATS

As with opportunities, I have divided the bitcoin threats into separate categories to be discussed in turn. These are:

1. Lack of demand
2. Competition
3. Legality
4. Deflation
5. Schism
6. Technical attacks

1. LACK OF DEMAND

The greatest threat to bitcoin's success is a lack of demand due to the availability of too many acceptable alternatives. The technology can be perfect and prices stable, but as long as people are happy with cash, credit cards and gold, bitcoin will not gain much significance. This is an unspectacular threat, but also one of the most underappreciated ones.

2. COMPETITION

Related to lack of demand, the appearance of a strong competitor is a slightly more interesting threat. First-movers often get replaced by new, superior systems – such as AltaVista by Google, MySpace by Facebook, or Hotmail by Gmail. Similarly, a new and better cryptocurrency might overtake bitcoin.

However, bitcoin has a huge lock-in, demanding significant improvements from competitors. There are many provable inferior technologies that we cannot get rid of even if there are known superior alternatives. Dvorak keyboards allow for faster typing then qwerty keyboards, the US has still not adopted the metric system, and the IPv6 protocol still has not replaced IPv4 even though it could resolve quite a few technical limitations (known as *pain points*) of today's internet. Thus, thanks to its head start bitcoin does not need to be afraid of competing cryptocurrencies that are not fundamentally better.

A much bigger risk than other cryptocurrencies are excellent commercial services such as Square that successfully conquer market segments otherwise covered by bitcoin.[18] Due to its static core, the bitcoin platform as it has been devised must either succeed in its current form or it will fail. An agile start-up with a good idea will always beat bitcoin when it comes to the ability to reinvent itself.

3. LEGALITY

The bitcoin community is very sensitive, if not paranoid, regarding legal questions. Many enthusiasts believe this threat to be the most relevant, although I do not share that view. Bitcoin is not regulated and generally the constitutional principle that everything not explicitly illegal is allowed applies. Obviously, that does not mean it is ok to use bitcoins for illegal activities. Stealing bitcoins is still theft and selling bitcoins without intent to actually deliver them is fraud.

In countries such as Switzerland and the United States, money laundering laws apply, requiring financial intermediaries handling bitcoins to follow guidelines such as the know-your-customer (KYC) rule. Funnily enough, the EU directive on money laundering had enough foresight to expressly take "electronic money" into account, but it uses such a narrow definition for electronic money that it does not apply to bitcoin.[19] Nonetheless, as a company, it is not advisable to bet on this legal loophole.

Even though the fears of bitcoin being illegal or getting outlawed are exaggerated, some concerns are justified. Similar to the spirit of the early internet, today's bitcoin economy resembles the Wild West. For example, unregulated exchanges allow for market manipulations outlawed long ago on stock markets[20] and gullible users are lured into dodgy investments that promise unrealistic returns.[21] Anything seems to be possible and a lot is being tried out – which is good.

Assuming it matures faster than lawmakers react, bitcoin does not have much to fear. For bitcoin to be outlawed, parliaments would need to get involved, which takes a lot of time and only happens if there is political pressure to do so. To avert this threat in the long run, bitcoin needs to win the hearts and minds of the public. The risk to be concerned about is not necessarily legality, but morality and perception. Bypassing the exorbitant fees of big finance is a good story. Being the currency of choice for avoiding taxes is not. To avert this risk, bitcoin must succeed in bringing substantial benefits in proper use cases.

4. DEFLATION

As often as critics are concerned with legal questions, they rule out bitcoin's success due to its inbuilt deflation.[22] There is no central bank or other entity in the bitcoin system that can alter money supply in order to stabilise prices. Assuming constant velocity,[23] the bitcoin exchange rate grows and shrinks with the bitcoin economy. As noted in the section 'Store of wealth', this allows holders of bitcoins to participate in its growth.

In the long term, this can indeed be detrimental as it curbs investment. If the bitcoin economy grows by 5% per year, hoarding bitcoins lets an investor already earn that return. Consequently, the same investor will not invest in other opportunities with an expected return of less than 5%. Thus, the limited supply of bitcoin can curb its growth. However, this is a luxury problem to have as it only occurs as long as there actually is growth. As soon as growth stops, the problem disappears. So, while detrimental to its success, long-term deflation poses no existential threat to bitcoin. After all, having the gold standard and accordingly only minimal inflation did not prevent the US from industrialising and growing significantly in the 19th century.[24]

In the short term, knowledge about limited supply can cause irrational speculation. Bitcoin speculators are often driven by self-reinforcing sentiments, which can lead to exuberance and panic. In the past, it was not uncommon to see short-term panics causing intraday drops and instant recoveries of 20% or even more.

Fortunately, the most emotional speculators are normally on the wrong side of the bet – making them lose money and influence over time. In fact, many amateur traders that panicked during the aforementioned price swings got burned and resorted to buy-and-hold strategies. As traders get more experienced and professional, short-term volatility will reduce. Even so, it should be accepted that bitcoin will probably never reach the stability of a currency controlled by a competent central bank in a stable economy.

5. SCHISM

One of the risks not unheard of in the open-source community is the occurrence of a severe dispute that ends in a schism. Imagine a faction of developers are concerned about deflation and demand an increase of the 21m bitcoin ceiling to 30m. In theory, this could be done if one manages to get the involved parties on board: programmers, miners (payment processors), merchants and end users.

Such a demand would split the community into inflationists and deflationists – each of them convinced they are right. If the inflationists succeed in gathering enough support, they could make the necessary changes to the software, convince enough end-users to switch to their version of bitcoin and enable the changes in a concerted effort. The result would be a so-called *blockchain fork*: the bitcoin network would split into two independent networks – one deflationist network that operated according to traditional rules and one inflationist network that operated according to the new rules. Both would have a common past but would diverge over time. A user owning 100 bitcoins before the split would own 100 deflationist bitcoins as well as 100 inflationist bitcoins after the split. He could start spending them independently.

A schism would severely damage bitcoin's reputation and by extension also its exchange rate. There are well-balanced incentives in place to avert such a scenario as long as a majority is rational and acting in their own self-interest. This reduces but does not eliminate the risk.

6. TECHNICAL ATTACKS

While being very innovative, bitcoin builds on proven cryptography, making fundamental technical attacks unlikely to be fruitful. The core system is well designed and has already been scrutinised by countless professionals. Notable successful attacks in the past have all exploited specific vulnerabilities of individual platforms or have been directed against services built on top of bitcoin.[25]

In one of the largest heists to date, over 43,000 bitcoins were stolen from Bitcoinica – a trading service that subsequently shut down its operations.[26] As another example, a specialised computer virus could irrevocably steal bitcoins stored on an infected computer. As painful as such attacks are to the individual victims, they do not pose a long-term threat to the system itself as the core is technologically sound.

EXCURSUS: COLLAPSE OF COMPLEX SOCIETIES

A dry SWOT analysis cannot convey the magic many associate with bitcoin. Bitcoin also has an ideological appeal which it draws from its cypherpunk anarcho-capitalism. There are many ways to look at the thinking behind this philosophy. Here, I'll concentrate on a scenario outlined in the highly recommended book *Collapse of Complex Societies* by anthropologist Joseph Tainter.

Tainter's book sheds light on one dimension of the deep distrust against centralised systems which is often encountered among bitcoin enthusiasts. His basic premise is that organisations tend to continuously increase in complexity, with decreases being very rare. New government bodies and regulations are created at a faster pace than they are abolished, leading to increasing overheads and an eventual collapse under the burden of maintaining a perpetually growing bureaucracy.

This is a process that can span over centuries of gradual decline – bringing to mind the well-known (but false) analogy of a frog getting boiled without noticing as the water around it warms up very slowly. Tainter's book describes various historical examples, including the downfall of the Roman Empire. As the number of laws and the size of the Roman administration increased over time, so did cost. The emperors resorted to reducing the amount of silver in newly minted coins from initially 92% to less than 5% over time, thereby inadvertently causing inflation.[27] In parallel, taxes increased decade by decade along with harsher laws being introduced. Near the empire's end, farmers sometimes had to sell their children into slavery in order to pay taxes. The benefits of the Roman Empire, such as stability, aqueducts and the rule of law, could not justify the high cost of maintaining it any more. The system collapsed and the dark ages followed.

There are numerous libertarians and anarcho-capitalists among bitcoin supporters who believe that Western society could suffer a similar fate: a gradual collapse due to the ever-growing burden of bureaucracy and centralism. Considering increasing centralisation of governmental power in Brussels, Washington and other capitals, regulatory frameworks getting denser and denser, and the decline of democratic principles such as a clean separation of powers, these pessimists might well be on to something. In the financial sector in particular, one can currently observe a vicious cycle of market failures and tighter regulations: due to dense regulation, running a financial institution comes with enormous overheads, forcing small players out of business or into mergers. This reduces competition, which again leads to more market failures, which politicians try to resolve through even tighter regulation.

Typically, it is during times of crisis that people start looking for alternatives. In 1932, amid the global economic depression, the Austrian city Wörgl decided to introduce their own local currency. They succeeded in reigniting the idle local economy, resulting in the Wonder of Wörgl. However, the experiment was stopped by the Austrian central bank.[28]

Today, people might resort to using bitcoin when faced with a similar loss in trust in conventional currencies. In 2013 monetary troubles in Argentina as well as the confiscation of bank accounts in Cyprus both lead to a surge in interest in bitcoin.[29] While bitcoin will not be able to avert the collapse of countries, it can offer a reliable monetary pillar in times of chaos. Comparable to the right to own gold, bitcoins can empower citizens by making them more independent from their sometimes dysfunctional governments.

CONCLUSION

Paul Krugman sees bitcoin as completely unnecessary.[30] He also said in 1998: "By 2005 or so, it will become clear that the internet's impact on the economy has been no greater than the fax machine's." I think he is wrong on both accounts. Bitcoin has the potential to profoundly shake up the way we perform transactions online and to finally deliver the internet currency Milton Friedman envisioned in 1999.[31]

As discussed in the opportunities section, bitcoin's value tends to increase the longer it exists. A currency needs trust and trust can only come with time. As the market matures and volatility declines, bitcoin gains in attractiveness. While I do not see much potential for offline payments, there is a good chance for bitcoin to gain relevance in online payments, including the often foretold micro-payments. Furthermore, its exceptionally strong property rights make bitcoin an excellent store of wealth that functions even under adverse conditions.

When it comes to threats, others are often concerned about deflation, legal risks and technical attacks. I deem those concerns secondary. The primary risk for bitcoin is a lack of demand beyond early adopters. It remains to be seen whether bitcoin can find a market niche where it can establish a beachhead to *cross the chasm from early adopters to early majority*, using the terms coined by Geoffrey Moore.[32] Along with that, it is important that morally positive use cases dominate over the undesirable or negative ones when it comes to winning the hearts and minds of the people.

Like the internet in its early days, bitcoin is currently in a stage resembling the Wild West. It provides a free and unclaimed territory to experiment with new and powerful ideas. This cannot be witnessed very often and comes both with exceptional chances as well as exceptional risk. In either case, it is worth observing. As a risk-taker, you might even want to hold a few bitcoins – just in case.

ENDNOTES

[1] 'Bitcoin: A Peer-to-Peer Electronic Cash System' by Satoshi Nakamoto, bitcoin.org/bitcoin.pdf; Post on the cryptography mailing list in which Satoshi announces Bitcoin and publishes the Bitcoin paper, www.mail-archive.com/cryptography@metzdowd.com/msg09959.html (1 November 2008); Satoshi releases version 0.1 of Bitcoin, announcement on the cryptography mailing list, www.mail-archive.com/cryptography@metzdowd.com/msg10142.html (9 January 2009).

[2] The term 'Bitcoin' on Google Trends, 31 July 2013, www.google.com/trends/explore?q=bitcoin

[3] Bitcoin relies on the widely used cryptographic standards ECDSA and SHA-256. In case they become obsolete, it is possible to switch to more secure (not yet invented) algorithms in future.

[4] Bitcoin Wiki on transaction fees: en.bitcoin.it/wiki/Transaction_fees

[5] Under the gold standard, central banks used to back their currencies with gold. This changed over the course of the 20th century, removing any hard limit for how much money a central bank can print.

[6] List of known businesses that accept Bitcoin: en.bitcoin.it/wiki/Trade

[7] Richard Falkvinge, 'Why I'm putting all my savings into Bitcoin' (29 May 2011), 'Bitcoin drivers part one: unlawful trade' (16 June 2011), 'Bitcoin drivers part two: international trade' (18 June 2011), 'Bitcoin drivers part three: merchant trade' (3 July 2011) and 'Bitcoin drivers part four: Investment' (5 July 2011). www.falkvinge.net

[8] A typical site created by a disgruntled PayPal customer: www.screw-paypal.com

[9] 'EU plan to cut credit and debit card fees is confirmed', BBC, www.bbc.co.uk/news/business-23431543 (24 July 2013).

[10] 'Credit card donations to WikiLeaks restored as Mastercard breaks ranks', *The Register*, www.theregister.co.uk/2013/07/05/wikileaks_credit_card_donations_restored (5 July 2013).

[11] 'Mega now accepts bitcoin payments', Wired www.wired.co.uk/news/archive/2013-02/19/mega-bitcoin (13 February 2013).

[12] 'SatoshiDice acquired in Bitcoin deal', iGaming Business, www.igamingbusiness.com/content/satoshidice-acquired-bitcoin-deal (22 July 2013). As of 2 August 2013 bets on BTC-Bet are 19 to 1 that Jez San, owner of pkr.com, was the buyer of Satoshi Dice.

[13] BitcoinTip: www.reddit.com/r/bitcointip

[14] Swiss National Bank, Cash Circulation: www.snb.ch/en/iabout/cash/id/cash_circulation

[15] (⅔ * 33bn CHF) / (21m Bitcoins) ≈ 1000 CHF ≈ 1000 USD

[16] Wikipedia on Proof-of-work: en.wikipedia.org/wiki/Proof-of-work_system

[17] 'Decentralized Cloud Exchange', BitcoinX, www.bitcoinx.org/about/the-technology.

[18] Square – the register reinvented, squareup.com.

[19] The directive requires electronic money to have an issuer that guarantees a value. Bitcoin has neither. This is typical flaw of overly detailed laws: in a perfectionist effort to control every detail, broad principles get lost. Directive 2009/110/EC, article 2, section 2: eur-lex.europa.eu/LexUriServ/LexUriServ.do?uri=OJ:L:2009:267:0007:0017:en:PDF

[20] An example would be "painting the tape", consisting of selling Bitcoins to oneself in order to artificially increase volumes and thus move volume-adjusted price indicators. See Investopedia on painting the tape: www.investopedia.com/terms/p/paintingthetape.asp

[21] Pirateat40 promised 7% weekly returns to anyone investing into his fund, en.bitcoin.it/wiki/Pirateat40.

[22] Typical comment on a tech forum (slashdot.org), yro.slashdot.org/comments.pl?sid=3802599&cid=43868677, Matt Yglesias (economics blogger), 'Bitcoin's Deflation Problem', www.slate.com/blogs/moneybox/2013/04/10/bitcoin_s_deflation_problem.html (10 April 2013), Bitcoin Wiki on deflationary spiral, en.bitcoin.it/wiki/Deflationary_spiral.

[23] Velocity is an economic measure of how often e.g. each dollar is spent per year. The higher the velocity of a currency, the less money needs to be in circulation to reach a given level of GDP. Wikipedia definition: en.wikipedia.org/wiki/Velocity_of_money

[24] While US prices fluctuated in the 19th century, they did not change much overall. From 1800 to 1900, the price index fell from 50 to 25, indicating slight deflation or a doubling of the purchasing power of the dollar. Between 1900 and 2000, the gold standard was abandoned and the price index rose to 517.5, inflating prices 20-fold. See Consumer Price Index (estimates) by the Federal Reserve Bank of Minneapolis, www.minneapolisfed.org/community_education/teacher/calc/hist1800.cfm.

[25] 'Android Security Vulnerability', Bitcoin.org (11 August 2013), bitcoin.org/en/alert/2013-08-11-android.

[26] Bitcoin Wiki on Bitcoinica, en.bitcoin.it/wiki/Bitcoinica, List of Bitcoin Heists, Bitcoin Talk. (28 July 2013), bitcointalk.org/index.php?topic=83794.0.

[27] Joseph Tainter, *Collapse of Complex Societies*, pp. 136-139.

[28] Das Wunder von Wörgl: www.zeit.de/2010/52/Woergl

[29] *Wall Street Journal* on surging interest in Bitcoin in Argentina, blogs.wsj.com/moneybeat/2013/07/17/bitcoin-downloads-surge-in-argentina, BBC on Bitcoin and Cyprus, www.bbc.co.uk/news/magazine-22292708.

[30] Paul Krugman, 'The Antisocial Network',
www.nytimes.com/2013/04/15/opinion/krugman-the-antisocial-network.html (15 April 2013).

[31] Milton Friedman on land tax and internet currencies,
www.youtube.com/watch?v=j2mdYX1nF_Y.

[32] Geoffrey A. Moore, 'Crossing the Chasm', en.wikipedia.org/wiki/Crossing_the_Chasm (1991).

MAKING HUMANS HAPPY

BY SIMON ROGERSON

ABOUT THE AUTHOR

Simon Rogerson is a co-founder and chief executive of Octopus Investments. Octopus was set up in 2000 to help people do smarter things with money. It is one of the fastest growing investment companies in the UK, with 50,000 retail investors and more than £3 billion under management. Octopus has twice been recognised as one of the best 100 smaller companies to work for and is one of only two investment companies to have ever been rated AAA in Citywire's Service Index.

INTRODUCTION

THERE'S ONE PARTICULAR interview question I ask which I think is quite telling:

"Which company do you most admire?"

Over the last five years, 70% of people have answered Apple, followed by Innocent Drinks, John Lewis and Google. No one, in the five years I've been asking this question (to thousands of candidates who have applied for a job at Octopus), has ever mentioned a financial services company.

Herein lies the opportunity – in a normal person's hierarchy of needs, money (as opposed to consumer electronics, smoothies, home furnishings or search engines) really matters. Fundamentally, financial services companies have the opportunity to change people's lives.

While there are dozens of reasons why financial services companies are falling short, the basic problem is that there's no connection between the customer and the company. Financial services companies are thought of as faceless organisations where individuals (employees as well as customers) are treated like numbers not people. Businesses that do this won't be admired. They will, at best, be tolerated.

This relationship aspect might sound soft, but it's the battleground for customers' hearts and minds. The firms which figure this out will absolutely win.

Over the course of this chapter, I'm going to set out what I consider to be five of the reasons for the breakdown in relationships between financial services companies and their customers. I'll use some examples of companies I think are getting it right (and wrong), and draw out some lessons that might be of use to those who are managing, or considering launching, their own financial services business.

LESSON 1: FOCUS ON THE CUSTOMER

In an industry dominated by brash, boastful and egotistical companies, the customer rarely comes first. For example, think about how financial services companies typically approach sales. Rather than take responsibility for the right product being sold to the right person, most firms sell down the path of least resistance.

Turn your mind back to 2000 or 2006. What do you suppose were the best-selling retail funds in those years? The answer is technology and commercial property funds respectively. Not because they were the best placed funds to deliver returns, but because they had performed very well in the prior three years and were therefore the easiest funds to sell.

The end result for investors in these funds was a loss of between 30% to 80% of their capital over the following three years. The decision the financial services companies made was to trade off long-term relationships in return for short-term profits. Ultimately, this shouldn't be sustainable because your customers should leave and your brand should suffer. I say "shouldn't be" rather than "isn't" because the level of financial literacy in the UK is currently very low, so companies get away with it.

The groundswell of ill-feeling towards financial services companies, and the growth of social media and the real-time impact that this can have, will hopefully change the status quo.

THE LESSON

Brands are built on insight. And you build insight by engaging with your customers, by building meaningful relationships where you'll get feedback into what is and isn't working.

Financial services companies rarely seem to understand this. So in the functional hierarchy that is so prevalent in investment companies (where the *investment professionals* take on god-like status in comparison to everyone else in the business), the functions that interact directly with the customer are largely ignored. Witness the merger between two large fund management companies where the customer service teams (for both the end investors and the financial advisers) were outsourced to a third party to save on cost.

The human equivalent of this would be for me to outsource my central nervous system to you. The only way I'll know I'm in pain is by asking you; I wouldn't feel any of the pain first-hand. The same is true in business. Customer-facing functions should be prioritised; they should be given a voice and the business should react quickly to their feedback.

LESSON 2: KEEP IT SIMPLE

The financial services industry, like the technology industry, is hideously complicated. Customers don't like this. Yet they invariably have no choice but to accept it.

Let's take an example from the technology sector to make the point. Advanced Technology Systems & Communications (ATSC) was a successful business selling bomb detection equipment to dozens of developing countries.

Its equipment was very high tech and worked on a principle of "electro magnetic ion attraction". Each of the handheld bomb detection units was fitted with "programmed substance detection cards", which allowed the units to detect different types of explosive.

Except they didn't. The whole company was a con. The antennas on the devices were actually car aerials and the "programmed substance detection cards" were the standard anti-theft tags found on clothing in stores. The device didn't even have a battery. The consequences were awful – thousands of people died when explosives went undetected.

The reason people fell for it was because people rarely question something as long as it has the credibility of technical-sounding language. People won't challenge something if they assume it's beyond their grasp; they rely on the fact that the product in question has been developed by someone more knowledgeable than them in that area.

James McCormick, the founder of ATSC, was sentenced to ten years in prison for fraud. He had another view of the equipment he sold and the way he sold it. He said "It did exactly what it was meant to do. It made money." Ring any bells with financial services? PPI insurance, mortgage backed securities or technology funds in 2000 for instance?

Financial services companies seem to delight in this world of jargon and complexity. There might be a few reasons for this – they might think that it makes them sound clever, they might be doing it (like ATSC) to appear to be something they're not, or they might be doing it because they can't relate to people outside of their own little bubble.

Here's a good example for you. A very large, traditional fund management company put in place one-page factsheets across its range of products for its direct investors. Over the course of one page, reference was made to correlation, alpha, the European Stability Mechanism and standard deviation. I'd wager that less than 1% of the company's customers (and probably less than 5% of the company's employees) knew what the factsheets were talking about.

THE LESSON

Use Winnie the Pooh English – short, simple sentences that everyone will understand. If customers can't understand what a business is communicating, they can't trust you.

That's why one of the Octopus sacred cows is the *Granny and Granddad Test*. This is a test we apply to all of our communications. If a granny or a granddad who has never worked in financial services wouldn't understand what we're communicating, it doesn't get sent out.

LESSON 3: ALWAYS HAVE A WHY

There are two things that great companies consistently do. The first is that they think about the needs of their customers before anything else. These needs include their functional needs as well as their emotional needs – an example being how an iPad makes you feel rather than what it actually does. The second is that great companies think, act and communicate in a totally different way to normal companies.

Exploring this last point, I think there are three layers to any business: the WHAT (the product or service you provide), the HOW (what's different about this product and service) and the WHY. The WHY is the reason you get out of bed in the morning. And here we're specifically not talking profit – profit should be the end result and not the driver.

Let's apply this logic to the legal profession as an example. Most legal firms start with the WHAT – "we provide expert legal advice you can depend on". Their HOW would sound something like "we've got some great lawyers and we act for 20 of the largest 50 companies in the UK". All of this is generic and could apply to any number of law firms. The problem is that there isn't a WHY. If really pushed, the WHY will probably come back to how much money the partners in the firm will make. That's not a backdrop to building great relationships. It means the relationship with the customers is transactional and superficial. There is no loyalty or connection so if another law firm provided the same service at a lower cost, customers would move immediately.

Great companies, however, approach customers in a totally different way. They start with the WHY. Great companies know exactly why they exist and how they're different. They have a purpose. Central to this purpose is the customer and their needs, both emotional and functional. This WHY is supported by every little detail – the HOW and the WHAT back it up at every touch point. This makes the company believable which, in turn, creates likeability.

This, to me, is why Apple is so ingenious. Apple has a very clear WHY – it sets out to challenge the status quo in everything it does. It wants to turn technology from something you hide away in a back room to something you want to show off to those around you. Every little bit of its business reflects this – from the design of its products to the layout of its stores, which are huge empty spaces with dozens of Apple employees to help you out, none of whom are paid sales commission.

Similarly, Apple doesn't feel the need to talk, or write, in techno babble, or to explain how all the little chips under the screen actually work. What they've done is to design something which is incredibly easy to use. There's a reason three-year-olds and 90-year-olds alike can use iPads (when they can't use other, simpler technology like printers). If you ever need to refer to the Apple instruction manual, you quickly realise that it's been written for a normal person rather than someone with a PhD in computer science.

THE LESSON

If you don't have a WHY, your relationships with your customers won't go beyond transactional.

In addition, your HOW must be equally as rewarding as your WHAT. Your process and your relationships must be as good as your product. Almost all financial services companies think that the WHAT is far more important than the HOW. It isn't. The tricky bit is that the HOW (the relationship) is a never ending process of a zillion moments of truth. The competition try to overcome this by commoditising the relationship and making it a cookie cutter process and in so doing they lose their personality.

You must remain real people who are interested in real people. And this comes from hiring the right people – people who are radiators not drains.

LESSON 4: DON'T PRETEND TO BE SOMETHING YOU'RE NOT

The corporate values of financial services companies are boringly predictable – integrity, customer service, excellence, winning. Trust is almost always there as well, which makes it all the more amusing when a bank then chains its pens to the table and places bulletproof glass between you and its staff.

The biggest problem with these values, however, is that they're just words. They're rarely used to assess candidates when recruiting and they're not seen as key influencers of behaviour inside the organisation.

So while businesses like Apple and Google have largely found a way to keep the integrity of their beliefs in spite of their growth and their size, financial services companies have failed.

Let's take one of the big high street banks in the UK as an example. This business is quite open in its ambition – it wants to be "one of the most valuable financial services companies in the world". They start, somewhat predictably, with themselves. They're focused on the result (their profit and their value) before everything else, including their customers. It would be foolish to suggest that companies are not money motivated, but the great ones will make profit the consequence of success, not the measure of it.

This bank then goes on to say that its values are "integrity, trust and behavioural excellence". The biggest problem here is that it isn't true. Their behaviour simply doesn't back this up. Their list of misdemeanours, including the recent LIBOR scandal, regulatory run-ins and the mis-selling of PPI insurance, continues to grow and people start to realise that their values are nothing more than an act. People don't like businesses which pretend to be something they're not.

What makes it worse is that this bank has no idea how to put it right. It's looking for someone to tell it what to do to be liked, so it focuses on "corporate social responsibility" or some other superficial veneer.

Bluntly, it has no hope of changing because the culture, the values and the behaviours all come from the people. And it's got the wrong people. It's got the wrong people because its hiring process prioritises functional ability over cultural fit. So it ends up with talented people but no unity. Every unit of energy is pulling in a slightly different direction.

THE LESSON

You need to create values which actually mean something and which stand out from the crowd. These values need to set out the kind of behaviours you're going to reward and similarly the kind of behaviours you won't accept. And you need to be true to these values at all times.

Nowhere is this more true than when you're hiring people. If you want to create the corporate equivalent of the Roman tortoise (the impenetrable shield formation soldiers created by fighting as a unit) then you need to hire people who genuinely share the same values.

When it's really obvious what you stand for, like-minded people (customers and potential employees) will seek you out. When you're surrounded by like-minded people and they all feel part of something together, you will achieve far more. Everyone will naturally head in the same direction. There will be very little wasted energy.

LESSON 5: GET THE BASICS RIGHT

There are few things more annoying in life than being taken for granted. I'll use two examples, at either end of the spectrum, to make my point.

At the terrible end, a story relating to one of the Octopus employees who was doing his weekly shop at his local supermarket. The cashier didn't acknowledge him. She simply scanned all his shopping and then announced how much it cost. No "Hello" and no "Please". The customer handed over his money and was handed back his change. No "Thank you" and no "Goodbye". The customer asked at the end if he was going to get a "Thank you". "Yes," came the reply, "it's printed at the bottom of your receipt".

At the other end of the spectrum is the story of a US supermarket chain. This chain, which was proud of its reputation for fresh produce, used to take the outer leaves off lettuces before putting them on display. One day, a shelf stacker suggested putting the leaves, which were binned, into bags given away free at the checkout for families whose children kept pet rabbits. They were called Bunny Bags and they couldn't give them away fast enough. Fifteen years later people still recall this.

THE LESSON

It's really simple. Set out to create likeability; people want to buy brands they like, that they feel are different and that are interested in them.

So put yourselves in the shoes of your customers. Show you care and that you're thinking of them. A simple thank you, for example, will work wonders. You absolutely want to be friends with people, and businesses, who say thank you. One of the best customer service success stories over the last ten years comes from a company which sells wine online in the US. The key to the company's success, according to its Chief Executive, is the fact that the first function he set up once he had a customer was a *thank you department*. Customers continue to be amazed that a business calls to say thank you; the result being that they have the highest repeat purchase rate of almost any online retailer.

Once you have the basics right, you can add the icing. These are the WOW moments that will turn your customers into ambassadors. A great example of this is provided by the airline Qantas. There was a flight to Australia which was in the air on Christmas day. So at 11:57pm on 24 December, the Captain turned on the lights in the plane and announced that air traffic control had been in touch and that they were expecting a visitor in a few minutes.

At 12am on 25 December, he took the plane off automatic pilot, wiggled the joystick and announced "He's landed". He then got dressed up as Santa Claus, emerged from the cockpit and walked the length of the plane delivering presents to the children on the flight. He then went back into the cockpit, took the plane off automatic pilot again and pointed the nose in the air to "help the reindeer take off again". This is the behaviour of a brand that you want to be friends with, where you want to tell others about what they've done. It wasn't difficult and it wasn't expensive. But it was personal and it showed they cared.

BRING BACK HUMANITY

The success of financial services businesses over the next decade will lie in the emotional proposition they offer their customers and that is about their tone of voice and their attitude (just as it is for businesses like Apple, Innocent Drinks and Virgin). Financial services are tough, brash, performance-based businesses (the absolute antithesis of a good service company). The new business models need to bring back humanity and choice and in doing so put the customer in charge. This emotional positioning will be evidenced by internal emails, the layout of the office and the type of people that these firms employ even before they get to formally communicating it to a wider audience.

Trust, which is the holy grail for financial services companies, is about having skin in the game. People trust you if you have something to lose. Making sure that customers know that you understand they have a choice is what will make you seem different. What makes people angry is their own impotence and this is aggravated by the swaggering and posturing of some of the current leaders in the financial services industry. The current financial services market is woefully short on choice, humanity and customer insight. This needs to change. The customer needs to come first and the WHY for each and every business needs to be all about making humans happy.

THE FUTURE IS ALL ABOUT THE DATA

BY CHRIS SKINNER

ABOUT THE AUTHOR

Chris Skinner is chairman of the Financial Services Club, CEO of Balatro Ltd. and comments on the financial markets through his blog the *Finanser*. He can be reached at chris.skinner@fsclub.co.uk.

ABSTRACT

THERE IS A range of trends impacting payments and transaction servicing that is culminating in radical changes to the whole way we think about banking and money. In part, these changes are being forced on the industry through regulatory agendas of politicians but, in larger part, these changes are being required by customers and corporates as technology changes relationships with their financial providers. This paper looks at the outcome of such changes and finds that financial institutions will be radically restructured around data assets within the next decade to cater for these new world needs.

THE INTERNET OF THINGS

During the past five years, almost every conference on banking and payments has talked about mobile and tablet computing. This is because everyone thinks mobile is the hot space today, which it is, but it won't be in the near future. Very rapidly, the device focused dialogue will move on to the *Internet of Things*.

This is the major disruption in the future technology landscape and here are the facts:

- The volume of internet traffic doubles every 18 months and is currently running at around two zetabytes, which is a trillion gigabytes. Most of it is video.
- The actual size of the internet doubles every 5.32 years.
- By 2020, there will be 50 billion devices connected to the internet, compared with 17 billion today.
- By 2020, there will be 6.58 devices per person using the internet, compared with 2.5 today.
- Nanotech is already here, with computers and cameras at sub-1mm sizes.
- Over 100,000 telephone masts are being built every year.
- The number of wifi units shipped has quadrupled in the last five years.
- Under IPv6, everyone on the planet can have up to 52 thousand, trillion, trillion web addresses.

So what?

The so what is that the mobile device focus was signalled as important to banking and payments over a decade ago. Now that mobile is here, we need to look for the next signal and that signal in the *Internet of Things*. This is the idea that in the near future the vast majority of our electronics will be connected to the internet and/or other nearby devices.

A refrigerator, for example, may have a touch screen on the door and be connected to the internet, allowing you to remotely access information such as what is in the fridge, its temperature and whether or not you have what you need to cook that spaghetti bolognese this evening. Another example is the Nest thermostat, which is a thermostat that allows you to remotely manage your house room temperatures using an app.

In years past, this idea was just an idea – something we said was coming. This year, however, was the first year when we could actually see the Internet of Things on display and it is clear that, within the next five years, we will be living in a world where almost every electronic device we own will be connected to something.

WHAT DOES THIS MEAN FOR TRANSACTION BANKING?

The Internet of Things means that the world will be augmented, such that wherever you go and whatever you are doing, your world can be supplanted by relevant, proactive, predictive, proximity-based information.

This concept was proposed many years ago when technology firms made a play for banks to deploy data warehouses to perform predictive analytics based upon consumer propensity models of their data-based behaviours. It may sound a little complex, but basically it was meant to use data patterns to predict what the customer would do next and whether they might need a new financial service.

A good example was analysis of purchases. If a client started to visit a store they had never been to before, such as Mothercare and the Early Learning Centre, this would indicate that something in their life is changing, in this case the arrival of a new family member being imminent. Therefore, the bank is provided with an opportunity to promote *baby bonds* for future education savings.

An alternative analysis might show behaviours that would indicate a house move, such as regular visits to a new town, and therefore a home buyers and movers package would be sent out in the post.

Obviously these approaches need to have the customer's permission, as promoting contextual services without permission is a breach of law, but the concept of contextual marketing has been bubbling within the payments industry for at least two decades.

Twenty years ago these predictive services were crude and based upon delayed responses that lagged the customer's behaviours, but were far ahead of their time as a concept. Today, this form of marketing combined with transaction is imperative as predictive marketing is the battleground of Big Data, and Big Data allows payments processors to be far more proactive rather than reactive.

A good example is shown with Google.

When Google knows that someone's searches are ideas, aspirations and needs, it can predict what is relevant to that person and target them precisely. If you search for *headache tablets side effects,* it might recommend that you switch to paracetamol and direct me via Google maps to my nearest pharmacist. If you search for *pricing TVs,* it might offer you a special deal with a retailer's discount code.

If you don't think that Google Analytics are the key to predictive, proactive marketing, just check out the results of research by three academics who found that Google predicts stock market movements pretty accurately:

"Debt" was the most reliable term for predicting market ups and downs, the researchers found. By going long when "debt" searches dropped and shorting the market when "debt" searches rose, the researchers were able to increase their hypothetical portfolio by 326 percent. (In comparison, a constant buy-and-hold strategy yielded just a 16 percent return.)[1]

In the same way, banks can use transaction data combined with search trends and other data to predict and then proactively offer a service in real time.

That service might be offering car loans as a customer drives past the showroom of the BMW dealership they were Googling last night or mortgages as they drive towards the real estate office of the broker found via search this morning.

Now that's all well and good, but it goes further than this as the prediction marketing can now be embedded into the Internet of Things.

This is well illustrated by the retail experience in grocery stores and has been built conceptually by Metro in Germany. Metro built a prototype of the grocery outlet of the future using NFC and RFID technologies. The concept store included the idea of dynamic pricing as you walk through the aisles, based upon your loyalty, shopping habits and more.

Your smartphone would send your preferences to the store's database as you entered such that you get special discounts on the items you buy most regularly. As you walk past these items, they change prices dynamically and your phone beeps a special discount deal today to alert you to these offers: *Just for you, buy one get one free (this offer is not available to anyone else instore).*

So you get the idea, but it goes one step beyond this.

As the Internet of Things means that everything has intel inside and *intellisense* becomes the competitive battleground using predictive, proactive marketing, you get combinations of deals coming together. The internet service provider, mobile carrier and bank can create a partnership with BMW where they are incentivised to encourage visits to BMW. As a result, you keep finding adverts, offers and deals all around you, as you are *intellisensed* for business in the virtual and physical world. It is the world evoked by that vision of Tom Cruise walking into the shopping mall in *Minority Report* and everything recognises him based upon his eye biometrics.

But forget the biometrics. We have this *intellisense* thanks to mobile wifi combined with RFID and NFC. This sensing of the presence of the payer and payee through the network can be seen in the use of mobile networks and apps.

For example, the Square Wallet and PayPal Instore apps are good examples of the evolving shape of retail payments, where transactions no longer involve any physical exchange of tokens, cards or paper, but purely a confirmation of the payment via the mobile network.

We are already living in a world where the Internet of Things is intelligently sensing our buying habits. This means the bank that ties itself into the value chain of *intellisense* is the bank that will be at the heart of the next generation of retail payments. And that means being the bank that mines data to provide predictive, proactive, proximity-based payments.

As mentioned, this is the world of the very near future and it is driven by the unrivalled momentum and rapid worldwide adoption of devices and a world where all hardware will be made smarter through not just the use of connected chipsets and next-generation parts, but also through the applications that add to their value.

The net:net of all of this is that banks and all firms will soon be focused upon wireless transaction processing through the net. In other words, rather than mobile payments and mobile banking that we talk about today, we will be talking about augmented payments and augmented banking tomorrow and, in that world, money is meaningless.

MONEY IS MEANINGLESS

Money is meaningless because we no longer deal in money. We deal in data.

The word *money* is usually associated with cash and, as most of us know, cash is no longer king, queen or even key, as all banks and card processors have a war on cash. We have a war on cash because we want to replace it with electronic processing that is cheaper and easier, and electronic processing means that cash becomes data. Money becomes meaningless because the data is what is important.

The problem with this view is that there is still a lot of cash around – it still represents over half of all payment volumes in most developed nations (see Figure 1). For example, even with all of the advertising for mobile and contactless in the UK, the 'Cash and Cash Machines Report 2013' shows that cash usage increased by around 10% for payments in the UK in 2012, with the number of cash payments (by businesses and individuals) up from 20.6 billion transactions per annum to 20.8 billion, representing more than half (54%) of all payments.

Figure 1 – cash is still the dominant form of payment

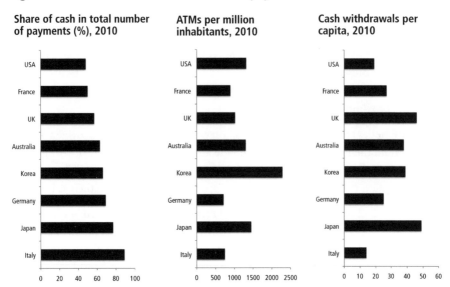

Source: McKinsey Payments Report 2012

But cash in the economy is going to decrease in importance over time, if for no other reason than the processors and financial institutions are all determined to displace cash with other forms of electronic payment.

In fact, the value of cash payments has been remaining steady in many economies, whilst the volume of cash transactions has been decreasing as alternative payment forms, such as contactless and mobile payments, take over (see Figures 2 and 3).

Figure 2 – non-cash payments are exploding, particularly card payments

(number of transactions per year in billions, estimated)

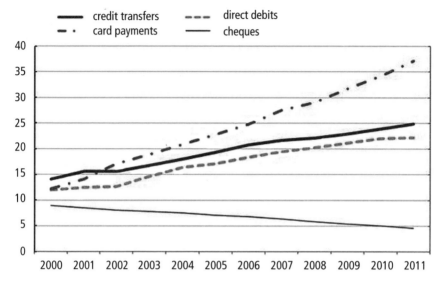

Source: ECB

Figure 3 – increasing numbers of mobile payments from 2008 to 2015

	2008	2009	2010	2011	2012	2013	2014	2015
Western Europe	2,015	4,519	9,471	18,451	29,243	41,310	56,139	73,915
North America	748	1,905	6,641	13,135	20,792	29,206	38,923	50,167
Asia/Pacific	26,418	41,865	55,265	69,091	83,327	97,896	112,784	127,804
EMEA*	9,119	16,823	25,127	34,250	44,289	55,471	67,473	80,899
Latin America	3,005	4,012	5,578	6,186	7,063	9,099	12,319	16,654
Total	41,305	69,124	102,083	141,112	184,714	232,983	287,638	349,440

*Does not include Western Europe

Source: Gartner

This brings us to the core point that cash will decline over time, replaced by electronic, digitised transactions. This is why money in the form of cash is less meaningful and demonstrates the importance of banks as secure data processors of money, rather than money transmissions processors.

It means that the regularly quoted comment from gangster Willie Sutton – "Why do you rob banks?", "Because that's where the money is." – is very last century. Willie Sutton robbed banks physically, taking the cash out at gunpoint. Today, the gangsters take the money out byte by byte.

Today it's the data that criminals need to steal, not the money. Data is where it's at.

That's why the majority of cyberattacks target financial institutions. According to RSA's December 2012 Online Fraud Report, 284 brands were targeted in phishing attacks during November 2012, marking a 6% decrease from October. Banks continue to be the most targeted by phishing, experiencing nearly 80% of all attack volumes.

Sophos regularly report details of bank cyberattacks, and McAfee Labs researchers recently debated the leading threats for the coming year and show that it's only going to get worse:

- Mobile worms on victims' machines that buy malicious apps and steal via tap-and-pay NFC.
- Malware that blocks security updates to mobile phones.
- Mobile phone ransomware that allows criminals without programming skills to extort payments.
- Covert and persistent attacks deep within and beneath Windows.
- Rapid development of ways to attack Windows 8 and HTML5.
- Large-scale attacks like Stuxnet that attempt to destroy infrastructure, rather than make money.
- A further narrowing of Zeus-like targeted attacks using the Citadel Trojan, making it very difficult for security products to counter.
- Malware that renews a connection even after a botnet has been taken down, allowing infections to grow again.
- The *snowshoe* spamming of legitimate products from many IP addresses, spreading out the sources and keeping the unwelcome messages flowing.
- SMS spam from infected phones. What's your mother trying to sell you now?
- Hacking as a Service: Anonymous sellers and buyers in underground forums exchange malware kits and development services for money.
- The decline of online hacktivists Anonymous, to be replaced by more politically committed or extremist groups.
- Nation states and armies will be more frequent sources and victims of cyberthreats.

So when we talk about our wonderful new internet age, the key is to realise that it's the data where the money is, not the bank, the branch or the cash machine.

This brings me to my core point: if data is valuable, what data is of most value and what role should banks take in this?

BANKS ARE JUST DATA VAULTS

Banks need to think about how they reconstruct themselves for the 21st century as new data management firms from upstart payments processors to internet service providers to mobile carriers all move towards the payments space. The war for all of these firms is to be the best at processing transaction data as people exchange information digitally online.

For a bank, what this really comes down to is that banks are becoming pure managers of bits and bytes of data. It is the data that has the value today and it is the data that is the basis of competitive battles in the future. Data is our greatest asset and raw material, not capital or people. That is what the technology has done for 21st century society and for 21st century banking.

Most people would be at far more of a loss if they lost access to their online accounts, had their usernames and passwords changed, had their identity copied and compromised online, or similar challenges, than if they lost their wallet or bank card.

For some, they would feel their lives were lost if their Facebook or Twitter accounts were blocked or deleted whilst, for others, their *World Of Warcraft* gold is more valuable to them than their total real world asset base.

The core of all of these discussions is data and data leverage.

By the same token, the data is where we have our greatest opportunity and threat. We talk about Apple, Amazon, Google and Facebook with admiration, but the core of these companies is not music, books, search and social networking. It's data management.

That is what Apple, Amazon, Google and Facebook have made of these businesses: massive data mining drones that allow us all to dump, tag, find, update and manage our online experience. This brings us back to the core themes of data being more important than money; that the Internet of Things will have us all drowning in even more data; that data access is our greatest vulnerability.

The themes all have one core point for traditional banks and payments firms, and that point of opportunity is that the bank of the 21st century is not a bank as we would recognise it at all. It's just a secure data vault.

The vulnerability of data, and hence the secure management of data, is where banks and processors can truly leverage their capabilities. If data is more important than money, then the bank that securely manages data is the bank that will win.

This is where the radical departure takes place from last century banking. Last century banking was predicated on money, paper and the physical transfer of goods. Banking in the 21st century is predicated on data, context, the electronic transfer of goods and, most of all, data security.

The biggest fear of corporates and consumers is that transactions will not be processed properly, that their bank access details might be compromised, that their data and therefore their money may be stolen. That is why banks have to step up to a big challenge: guaranteeing data security. Banks of the 21st century need to be bold and guarantee customer data is secure.

The issue with this is that it would make the processor or the bank a target for hackers, but that is the exact point. Banks should beat the hackers at their own game and make bold claims, such as *we guarantee your money* and *your data is 100% safe with us*. After all, if banks or their partners don't do this, who will?

According to many in the industry, banks and their payments processing partners are not positioned to do this. In fact, some believe that banks should leave secure data management to people who know how to do this, such as Google and PayPal.

This is where the biggest future weakness lies if this is the attitude of the financial community. If you give Google or PayPal the opportunity to become the secure financial data manager or the secure data vault of everything, then what is the role of the processor and the bank in that future? Surely this just gives the whole game away to someone else?

This is why the focus upon data and data security is the key to the future. It is not a focus upon money and financial security, but data and information security that will differentiate the future winners and losers.

In the meantime, banks have to transition from the old world of physical monetary security to this new world of electronic data security. There is a transition time between the old world and the new, and the question is for how long this transition is going to take place. A decade? Or two? A year? Or two? Now?

By way of illustration, if you look at the new world, there are already many different models of payments and banking emerging. On the one hand, you have visionary financial services providers – Moven, Simple, Gobank, Bluebird, Fidor, Jibun et al – pushing the envelope of being vaults for secure data. Their premise is that the leverage of data and the knowledge they can gather from your data allows these firms to improve the value you receive from your shared electronic relationship. It's context, proximity, location-based proactive servicing of data value that these banks offer, and that is how they will flourish and grow.

There are other new models of finance emerging such as Zopa, Friendsurance, eToro and more, that will change the game again. These providers are all seeking to connect people and money through social mechanisms, and base their business upon seeing new niche opportunities for managing the exchange of data value.

Finally, we see a few hybrid banks emerging such as Alior and mBank in Poland, which offer the mixed old and new world capabilities to reach the broadest audience with the deepest relationships. Both of these are traditional banks with branches that have rebranded and relaunched as hybrid banks, incorporating social data security with bank data security.

In all of these models, the core financial offers focus upon being the best at offering a remote, digital bank service that is fully secured and private. In other words, the best data vaults for money and more.

DATA IS THE CORE

In conclusion, and as demonstrated, the future is all about pervasive electronic connectivity. With such ubiquitous connectivity of everything from shoes to walls, doors to cars, windows to fridges, we will see non-stop capabilities for leveraging data assets for sales and servicing.

The contextual capability to market and target consumers and corporates at their point of need is going to be the battleground for future transaction processors, and those that not only leverage their data assets effectively but do this securely will be the companies that win.

ENDNOTE

---

[1] *Quantifying Trading Behavior in Financial Markets Using Google Trends* by *Tobias Preis*, of Warwick Business School, *Helen Susannah Moat*, of University College London, and *H. Eugene Stanley*, of Boston University, Nature Publishing Group's Scientific Reports, April 2013.